ALSO BY MARK R. LEVIN

*The Liberty Amendments*
*Ameritopia*
*Liberty and Tyranny*
*Rescuing Sprite*
*Men in Black*

# PLUNDER
## AND DECEIT

BIG GOVERNMENT'S EXPLOITATION
OF YOUNG PEOPLE AND THE FUTURE

## Mark R. Levin

THRESHOLD EDITIONS

New York   London   Toronto   Sydney   New Delhi

Threshold Editions
An Imprint of Simon & Schuster, Inc.
1230 Avenue of the Americas
New York, NY 10020

First Threshold Editions paperback edition July 2016

THRESHOLD EDITIONS and colophon
are trademarks of Simon & Schuster, Inc.

For information about special discounts for bulk purchases,
please contact Simon & Schuster Special Sales at
1-866-506-1949 or business@simonandschuster.com.

The Simon & Schuster Speakers Bureau can bring authors to your
live event. For more information or to book an event, contact the
Simon & Schuster Speakers Bureau at 1-866-248-3049 or visit our
website at www.simonspeakers.com.

Manufactured in the United States of America

10 9 8 7 6 5 4 3

Library of Congress Cataloging-in-Publication Data is available.

ISBN 978-1-4516-0633-1
ISBN 978-1-4516-0630-0 (HC)
ISBN 978-1-4516-0640-9 (ebook)

*To My Beloved Family, Fellow Countrymen,*
*and Future Generations*

# Contents

# CONTENTS

# PLUNDER AND DECEIT

ONE

## PLUNDER AND DECEIT

*Children sweeten labours, but they make misfortunes*
*more bitter: they increase the cares of life, but*
*they mitigate the remembrance of death.*
—British philosopher and statesman Sir Francis Bacon[1]

CAN WE SIMULTANEOUSLY LOVE our children but betray
their generation and generations yet born?

Among the least acknowledged facts of American modernity is the extent to which parents, acting in their familial
capacity, naturally and tenaciously guard their young children
from threat and peril, to the point of risking their own physical and economic security in extreme cases; however, as part
of the political and governing community—that is, the *ruling
generation*—many of these same parents wittingly and unwit-
tingly join with other parents in tolerating, if not enthusiastically championing, disadvantageous and even grievous public
policies that jeopardize not only their children's future but the
welfare of successive generations. To be clear, not all parental

decisions are impactful or consequential in the lives of children; obviously, not all decisions are equal. Indeed, the most attentive and nurturing parents are not and cannot be conscious of every decision they make inasmuch as the totality of such decisions is likely incalculable even on a weekly or monthly basis. Moreover, in the healthiest families, the most considered parental decisions, based on seemingly prudential judgments, can and do produce unintended consequences. Of course, the same can be said of decisions about public policy and governing in a relatively well-functioning community.

However, there are accepted norms of behavior, a *moral order*—born of experience and knowledge, instinct and faith, teaching and reason, and love and passion—that provide definition for and boundaries between right and wrong, good and evil, and fairness and injustice, applicable to families and societies alike. Hence, a harmony of virtuous interests, informed by tried-and-true traditions, customs, values, and institutions, and cultivated within families and the larger community, preserves and improves the human condition, one individual at a time, and one generation to the next. Broadly speaking, this is the *civil society*.[2]

Edmund Burke, a political thinker who was born in Ireland and moved to England, where he became a prominent statesman in the eighteenth century, explained that the civil society relies on an intergenerational continuum of the past, the living, and the unborn. He wrote that "as the end of such a partnership cannot be obtained in many generations, it becomes a partnership not only between those who are living but between those who are dead, and those who are to be born."[3] In fact, Burke went further, warning that those who forsake the intergenerational continuum condemn themselves, their children, and future generations to a grim existence. "One of the first and most leading principles on which the commonwealth and the laws are consecrated is, lest the temporary possessors and life-renters in it, unmindful of what they have received from their ancestors or of what is due to their posterity, should act as if they were the entire masters, that they should not think it among their rights to cut off the entail or commit waste on the inheritance by destroying at their pleasure the whole original fabric of society, hazarding to leave to those who come after them a ruin instead of a habitation—and teaching these successors as little to respect their contrivances as they had themselves respected the institutions of their forefathers."[4]

History confirms Burke's observation. To embrace the moral order as parents nurturing their children, yet to abandon the moral order as members of the ruling generation, thereby contributing to predictably deleterious public policies with prospectively calamitous outcomes, is a decadence that leads to unstable and potentially oppressive or even tyrannical conditions which, in the end, degrade and disassemble the civil society and consume their children's generation and generations beyond. Reformation and recovery may be possible but difficult and complicated, and typically only after the exaction of an enormous human toll.

Burke's commentary was motivated by his reflections on the decade-long French Revolution and his revulsion at the anarchy and horror it unleashed. In the ensuing more than two centuries, and up to this very moment, the world has witnessed much worse. This is not to say that all instances of civil and societal dislocation take the form of bloody revolution or civil war. Obviously, there are varying pathologies peculiar to particular doctrines, cultures, governing systems, and so on. There are also differing events and circumstances, some building over time and others descending more abruptly, that contribute to the character of the discontinuity. But violence is the ultimate exposure.

Before Burke, Charles de Montesquieu, a French philosopher whose life predated the American Revolution but who was hugely influential on the Constitution's Framers, also wrote of the disastrous aftermath of the civil society's abandonment. He explained: "When that virtue ceases, ambition enters those hearts that can admit it, and avarice enters them all. Desires change their objects: that which one used to love, one loves no longer. One was free under the laws, one wants to be free against them. Each citizen is like a slave who has escaped from his master's house. What was a *maxim* is now called *severity*; what was a *rule* is now called *constraint*; what was *vigilance* is now called *fear*. There, frugality, not the desire to possess, is avarice. Formerly the goods of individuals made up the public treasury; the public treasury has now become the patrimony of individuals. The republic is a cast-off husk, and its strength is no more than the power of a few citizens and the license of all."[5]

In modern America, the unraveling of the civil society had been subtly persistent but is now intensifying. Evidence of rising utopian statism—the allure of political demagogues and self-appointed masterminds peddling abstractions and fantasies in pursuit of a nonexistent paradisiacal society, and the concomitant accretion of governmental power in an increasingly authoritarian and centralized federal Leviathan—abounds. As subsequent chapters will demonstrate, the ruling generation's governing policies are already forecast to diminish the quality of life of future generations. Among other things, witness the massive welfare and entitlement state, which is concurrently expanding and imploding, and the brazen abandonment of constitutional firewalls and governing limitations. If not appropriately and expeditiously ameliorated, the effects will be dire. And the ruling generation knows it.

An August 2014 *Wall Street Journal*/NBC poll found that "Americans are registering record levels of anxiety about the opportunities available to younger generations and are pessimistic about the nation's long-term prospects, directing their blame at elected leaders in Washington. . . . [S]eventy-six percent of adults lack confidence that their children's generation will have a better life than they do—an all-time high. Some

71% of adults think the country is on the wrong track . . . and 60% believe the U.S. is in a state of decline. . . . This widespread discontent is evident among just about every segment of the population. Fifty-seven percent of those polled said that something upset them enough to carry a protest sign for one day. That included 61% of Democrats and 54% of Republicans, as well as 70% of adults who identify with the tea party and 67% of self-described liberals."[6]

It is past time and, therefore, imperative that the ruling generation acquaints itself with James Madison's uncomplicated and cautionary insight, written to bolster the proposed Constitution's ratification at the state conventions. In *Federalist 51*, Madison explained the essential balance between the civil society and governmental restraint: "But what is government itself, but the greatest of all reflections of human nature? If men were angels, no government would be necessary. If angels were to govern men, neither external nor internal controls on government would be necessary. In framing a government which is to be administered by men over men, the great difficulty lies in this: you must first enable the government to control the governed; and in the next place oblige it to control itself."[7]

However, why do so many loving parents, as part of the ruling generation, abandon the civil society for the growing tyranny of a voracious central government that steals their children's future, thus condemning their children and unborn generations to a dangerously precarious and unstable environment, despite a large majority acknowledging the national decline for which they blame politicians?

There are a number of possibilities. For example, language itself can contribute to the problem. The words "generation" and "ruling generation" and "future generations" can be imprecise and, for some, elusive. They can be thought of as merely theoretical and conceptual, or an unreality. Hence, the growth of numerous offshoots intended to provide context and clarification: Baby Boomers, Generation X, Millennials, Generation Z, etc. That said, it is neither my purpose nor my desire to give them each exposition and fill these pages with distractions about sociological constructs.

Nonetheless, despite inexact nomenclature, there are differences relating to various age groups, some big and others inconsequential, just as there are similarities and shared interests. This is also true of individuals generally. More to the point, and importantly, parents are constantly thinking about and talking about their own children, and interacting with them in their everyday lives. Obviously, children are of flesh and blood, and their existence and condition are reality. Given that the future is not the here and now and future generations are images or ideas of amorphous groups of strangers, born and unborn, parents can delude themselves that their own children's immediate welfare, which they work to protect and improve, can be detached from the well-being of future generations.

This psychology also makes it easier for parents, as part of the ruling generation, to downplay or ignore the longer-term and broader ruinous effects of contemporary public policies and reject any role or responsibility in contributing to them. It is a contradiction that usually originates with governing elites and statists, who relentlessly reinforce and encourage it. They self-righteously advocate public policies that obligate future generations' labor and resources to their own real and perceived benefit, empowering governmental abuse via social engineering and economic depredation. They disguise the delinquency as compassionate and premised on good intentions, often insisting their objectives will improve the prospects of those most severely burdened by them—"the children." Moreover, the mastermind's tactics are disarming if not seductive. As I wrote in *Ameritopia*, "[w]here utopianism is advanced through gradualism . . . it can deceive . . . an unsuspecting population, which is largely content and passive. It is sold as reforming and improving the existing society's imperfections and weaknesses without imperiling its basic nature. Under these conditions, it is mostly ignored, dismissed, or tolerated by much of the citizenry and celebrated by some. Transformation is deemed innocuous, well-intentioned, and perhaps constructive but not a dangerous trespass on fundamental liberties."[8]

Certainly, not all parents or members of the ruling generation downplay or disregard the soaring costs and heavy burdens of scores of public policies on their children and future generations. Many are acutely aware of the gathering storm of societal and economic disorder and wish to do something about it. For them, the difficulty lies in not knowing how to effectively influence the omnipresence and complexity of a massive governing enterprise that is less republican and more autocratic, an ambitious project indeed. The masterminds and their flatterers are progressively immune to regular democratic processes and pressures, such as elections and citizen lobbying, unless, of course, the electoral results and policy demands comport with their own governing objectives. Otherwise, they have an escalating preference for rule by administrative regulation, executive decree, and judicial fiat as the ends justifies the means.

Many in the ruling generation have themselves become entrapped in economically unsustainable governmental schemes in which they are beneficiaries of and reliant on public programs, such as unfunded entitlements, to which they have contributed significantly into supposed "trust funds" and around which they have organized their retirement years. They also find self-deluding solace in the politically expedient and deceitful representations by the ruling class, which dismisses evidence of its own diversion and depletion of trust funds and its overall maladministration as the invention of doomsayers and scaremongers.

In his two-volume masterpiece *Democracy in America*, French historian and scholar Alexis de Tocqueville, writing about the species of despotism that might afflict America, observed: "Our contemporaries are constantly excited by two conflicting passions: they want to be led, and they wish to remain free. As they cannot destroy either the one or the other of these contrary propensities, they strive to satisfy them both at once. They devise a sole, tutelary, and all-powerful form of government, but elected by the people. They combine the principle of centralization and that of popular sovereignty; this gives them a respite; they console themselves for being in tutelage by the reflection that they have put in leading-strings, because he sees that it is not a person or a class of persons, but the people at large who hold the end of his chain. By this system the people shake off their state of dependence just long enough to select their master and then relapse into it again."[9]

Thus mollified, many in the ruling generation are by and large inattentive and heedless about the bleak prospects inflicted on younger people, who will neither benefit from the government's untenable programs, into which they are or will also be forced to make "contributions," nor possess the wherewithal to pay the trillions of dollars in outstanding accumulated debt when the amassed IOU bubble bursts during their lifetimes or the lifetimes of future generations. Still, it is argued that millions of people benefit from such programs. Of course, trillions of dollars in government expenditures over many years most assuredly benefit the recipients of subsidies or other related payments. But this does not change the arithmetic. The eventual collapse of a colossal government venture will indiscriminately engulf an entire society and economy, including its millions of beneficiaries and benefactors, resulting in widespread disorder and misery. While this alone is daunting, no less derelict and pernicious are the other seemingly myriad ideological pursuits and social designs loosed on society by a ubiquitous federal government.

There is no comparable corporate structure shoring up the civil society and counterbalancing the federal government's discrediting and impositions. The federal government makes, executes, and adjudicates the laws. It even determines the extent to which it will comply with the Constitution, which was established in the first place to prevent governmental arrogation. Oppositely, the civil society does not possess mechanical governing features that, at the ready, can be triggered and deployed in its own defense. Ultimately, a vigorous civil society and a well-functioning republic are only possible if the people are virtuous and will them.

Therefore, what parents and the ruling generation owe their children and generations afar are the rebirth of a vibrant civil society and restoration of a vigorous constitutional republic, along with the essential and simultaneous diminution of the federal government's sweeping and expanding scope of power and its subsequent containment. If the ruling generation fails this admittedly complicated but central task, which grows ever more difficult and urgent with the passage of time and the federal Leviathan's hard-line entrenchment, then the very essence of the American experiment will not survive. As such, it can and will be rightly said that the ruling generation betrayed its posterity.

But what will be said of the younger generation—that is,

the *rising generation*—say, young adults from eighteen to thirty-
five years of age, if their response to the mounting tyranny of
centralized, concentrated governing power is tepid, contribu-
tory, or even celebratory? Do they not wish to be a free and
prosperous people? Do they not have a responsibility to preserve their own well-being and that of subsequent generations
by resisting societal mutation and economic plunder?

The rising generation seems wedged in its own contra-
dictions. While it is said to distrust ambitious authority and
question the so-called status quo, further examination suggests that in large numbers its members sanction both through
their political behavior and voting patterns. Although they
self-identify as political independents, Pew Research reports
that the rising generation "vot[es] heavily Democratic and for
liberal views on many political and social issues," including "a
belief in an activist government." Furthermore, when asked
"would you say that most people can be trusted or that you
can't be too careful in dealing with people, just 19% . . . say
most people can be trusted."[10] But what is activist government if not trust in a relative handful of political masterminds
exercising extraordinary power and commanding a large army
of civil servants to manage the lives of millions of individuals? Paradoxically, there is no age group more enthusiastically
reliable and committed by political deed to an activist if not
fervent governing elite than the rising generation, and no age
group more jeopardized by it.

Anomalies can be difficult to unravel; however, a few observations are merited. As a general and logical matter, younger people's dearth of life experiences and their quixotic idealism make them especially vulnerable to simplistic appeals and emotional manipulation for utopia's grandiosity and social causes, which are proclaimed achievable only through top-down governmental designs and social engineering and, concurrently, the detachment from and deconstruction of societal traditions, customs, and values, for which they have little or modest conception and investment. Consequently, while in the main and abstractly the rising generation may be distrustful of authority and people, younger people are also especially susceptible to seduction by demagogic politicians, propagandizing academics, charismatic cultural idols, and other authority and popular figures propounding splendid notions of aggressive government activism for and through such corresponding militant causes as "social justice," "environmental justice," "income equality," and other corollaries of radical egalitarianism.

In *Liberty and Tyranny*, I explained that this way of thinking "all but ignores liberty's successes in the civil society in which humans flourish, even though [we are] surrounded in [our] every moment by its magnificence. . . . Liberty's permeance in American society often makes its manifestations elusive or invisible to those born into it. Even if liberty is acknowledged, it is often taken for granted and its permanence assumed. Therefore, under these circumstances, the Statist's agenda can be alluring. . . . It is not recognized as an increasingly corrosive threat to liberty but rather as co-existing with it."[11]

Inasmuch as the proclaimed injustices and imperfections of the civil society are presumably illimitable, so are the infinite reactionary governmental prescriptions and interventions allegedly required to abate them. Therefore, government activism and social designs in this context are perceived as routine, indispensable, and noble. However, the erosion of individual sovereignty, free will, and self-sufficiency necessarily give way to dependence, conformity, and finally tyranny.

Although the pattern is not unique to the rising generation, younger people often find self-esteem, purpose, passion, and, frankly, coolness when associated with or devoted to causes and movements self-proclaimed as righteous or even sacred. Eric Hoffer, the brilliant longshoreman philosopher, writing about the nature of mass movements, declared: "The prime objective of the ascetic ideal preached by most movements is to breed contempt for the present. . . . The very impracticability of many of the goals which a mass movement sets itself is part of the campaign against the present."[12]

These utopian causes and movements are evinced by demands for assorted forms of expanded statism—increased governmental usurpations and empowerment—which invariably contribute to the deterioration of the civil society. To be clear, however, the rising generation is among the most devoted advocates of activist government. Consequently, it cannot be said to rebel against authority, although its members may believe that they do, but sanction its exercise and abuse in an incrementally severe centralized government, the latter of which, and its effects, have steadily emerged as the predominant characteristic of the actual status quo.

In particular, undergirding the rising generation's ethos in this regard is the relentless indoctrination and radicalization of younger people, on a daily basis and over the course of many years, from kindergarten through twelfth grade to higher education in colleges and universities, which engrains within them a vulnerability to exploitation and zealotry. It builds among them acceptance or even clamor for self-destructive policies and conditions that ensure future economic and political instability.

Even the most diligent parents have little effective input into what their children are taught in these classrooms. Indeed, they have no adequate or routine influence in the selection of teachers and professors, curriculum, or textbooks, which principally advance, either openly or through insinuation, a statist agenda and ideological groupthink hostile to the civil society and the American heritage. The immunization of formal education from parental and community input is a monumentally disastrous event. Professor Bruce Thornton of California State University observes that the project is deceitful and insidious: "The founding of the United States . . . was not about things like freedom and inalienable rights, but instead reflected the economic interests and power of wealthy white property-owners. The civil war wasn't about freeing the slaves or preserving the union, but about economic competition between the industrial north and the plantation south. The settling of the West was not an epic saga of hardships endured to create a civilization in a wilderness, but genocide of the Indians whose lands and resources were stolen to serve capitalist exploitation. Inherent in this sort of history were the assumptions of Marxist economic determinism and the primacy of material causes over the camouflage of ideals and principles."[13]

In fact, Thornton's point about the perversion of formal education as a format for class warfare proselytizing is the modern American version of a central theme in *The Communist Manifesto*. Its authors, Karl Marx and Friedrich Engels, argued: "The history of all hitherto existing society is the history of class struggles."[14] They continued, "Freeman and slave, patrician and plebeian, lord and serf, guild master and journeyman, in a word, oppressor and oppressed, stood in constant opposition to one another, carried on an uninterrupted, now hidden, now open fight, that each time ended, either in the revolutionary reconstitution of society at large, or in the common ruin of the contending classes."[15]

By cultivating agitation and balkanization almost nothing about the civil society is said to be true, right, or lasting and, therefore, worth preserving and perpetuating. Instead, much uproar is generated in the quest for utopian abstractions and societal transformation—the fundamental cause around which younger people have been encouraged and trained to rally, to their detriment and the jeopardy of subsequent generations, and to the benefit of the statist.

The ominous signs of the rising generation's imperilment from these ideological contrivances are already abundant. For example, respecting contemporary social and economic conditions, Pew Research reports that today's younger people "are . . . the first in the modern era to have higher levels of student loan debt, poverty and unemployment, and lower levels of wealth and personal income than their two immediate predecessor generations had at the same stage of their life cycles."[16] Specifically, at the end of 2012, individuals under 40 had $645 billion in student loan debt, an increase of 140 percent since 2005.[17] In 2014, unemployment for individuals between the ages of 16 and 19 hovered around 20 percent[18] and the underemployment rate for recent college graduates stood at 46 percent.[19] Among those aged 25 to 32 today, 22 percent with only a high school diploma are living in poverty compared to 7 percent of individuals aged from approximately 49 to 67 years of age who had only a high school diploma in 1979 when they were in their late twenties and early thirties.[20]

In a separate study, Pew also found that "Young adults ages 25 to 34 have been a major component of the growth in the population living with multiple generations since 1980—and especially since 2010. By 2012, roughly one-in-four of these young adults (23.6%) lived in multi-generational households, up from 18.7% in 2007 and 11% in 1980."[21]

Furthermore, the Congressional Budget Office (CBO),
an appendage of Congress, reports that without a dramatic
change in federal government spending, "[t]wenty-five years
from now . . . federal debt held by the public [will] exceed
100 percent of GDP. . . . [D]ebt would be on an upward path
relative to the size of the economy, a trend that could not
be sustained indefinitely." In addition, "[b]eyond the next
25 years, the pressures caused by rising budget deficits and debt
would become even greater unless laws governing taxes and
spending were changed. With deficits as big as the ones that
CBO projects, federal debt would be growing faster than GDP,
a path that would ultimately be unsustainable." The CBO
concludes: "At some point, investors would begin to doubt the
government's willingness or ability to pay its debt obligations,
which would require the government to pay much higher interest costs to borrow money. Such a fiscal crisis would present
policymakers with extremely difficult choices and would probably have a substantial negative impact on the country. Even
before that point was reached, the high and rising amount of
federal debt that CBO projects under the extended baseline
would have significant negative consequences for both the
economy and the federal budget."[22]

Thomas Jefferson presciently warned against such immoral collective behavior: "We believe—or we act as if we
believed—that although an individual father cannot alienate
the labor of his son, the aggregate body of fathers may alienate
the labor of all their sons, of their posterity, in the aggregate,

and oblige them to pay for all the enterprises, just or unjust, profitable or ruinous, into which our vices, our passions or our personal interests may lead us. But I trust that this proposition needs only to be looked at by an American to be seen in its true point of view, and that we shall all consider ourselves unauthorized to saddle posterity with our debts, and morally bound to pay them ourselves; and consequently within what may be deemed the period of a generation, or the life of the majority."[23] A few years later, Jefferson expressed even more trepidation: "[With the decline of society] begins, indeed, the *bellum omnium in omnia* [the war of all against all], which some philosophers observing to be so general in this world, have mistaken it for the natural, instead of the abusive state of man. And the fore horse of this frightful team is public debt. Taxation follows that, and in its train wretchedness and oppression."[24]

The laws of economics, like the laws of science, are real, unlike the utopian images and empty assurances of expedient and self-aggrandizing politicians and bureaucrats. There is a point of irreversibility from which no generation and the larger society can recover. Moreover, just as economic and political liberty are intertwined, spreading economic instability leads to political turmoil and, ultimately, societal disorder or collapse. In the interim, as this process unfolds, the dissolution of constitutional republicanism—including representative and consensual governance, dispersed authority among federal branches and between the federal and state govern-

ments, and the empowerment of a pervasive federal administrative state incessantly insinuating itself into the lives of the
people—becomes regular and routine. The ensuing amalgama-
tion of governmental control, and the escalating police powers discharged to coerce and subjugate the individual through
multitudinous rules, regulations, taxes, fines, and penalties,
confounds and benumbs much of the citizenry. Furthermore,
the designed societal transformation and decay of enlightened
self-government are portrayed as compassionate, progressive,
and inevitable.

Nonetheless, the federal colossus will not reform itself and
self-surrender its design. Its advocates, surrogates, and beneficiaries neither admit failure nor entertain circumspection.
They are increasingly fanatical as they insist on more zealous
applications of their ideological preoccupations and societal
schemes.

The time is urgent for the ruling generation and the rising generation—that is, parents and their progeny—to step
up in defense of their joint interests and in opposition to their
common foe—a government unmoored from its constitutional
beginnings and spinning out of control. The statist abuses and
exploits younger people and subsequent generations, expro-
priating the fruits of their labor and garnishing wealth yet created, as a cash cow for voracious, contemporary governmental
plundering, and manipulating and constricting their prospects
and liberty even before they are of age to more fully pursue
and enjoy them. The ruling generation, upon sober reflec-

tion, must stir itself to action in order to untangle the web of societal and generational conflicts produced by the statists' endless and insidious social engineering and encroachment, even though it requires some level of economic self-sacrifice and partial withdrawal from governmental entitlements and subsidies.

The equally formidable struggle for younger people is first to recognize the constant and self-reinforcing influences of statist manipulation and exploitation, break loose from them, and then rally against them in their own defense. The rising generation must question, confront, and civilly resist the real authoritarianism that endangers its future and the quality of life of those not yet born, whether preached in the classroom, popularized through entertainment, or idealized by demagogic politicians. Their well-being as a free, self-sufficient, and thriving people is at stake. The real fight they must wage is against utopian statism, which grows at the expense of the civil society and their own security and happiness. Otherwise, the rising generation—and unborn, unrepresented generations that follow—will degenerate into a lost and struggling generation, living an increasingly bleak and hollow existence under steadily more centralized, managed, and repressive rule.

At the beginning of this chapter I asked: Can we simultaneously love our children but betray their generation and generations yet unborn? The answer is no. I also asked: Do younger people wish to be free and prosperous? Do they have a responsibility to preserve their own well-being and that of subsequent generations by resisting societal mutation and economic plunder? The answer to both questions is yes. It turns out that the ruling and the rising generations have much in common after all.

In the first place and in the end, we must rely on our individual and collective capacity, albeit imperfect and fallible, for sound judgment and right reason. There are eternal and unchangeable universal truths that no professor, politician, expert, or combination thereof can alter or invalidate. The mission of this book, as in my past books, is to persuade as many fellow citizens as possible, through scholarship, facts, and ideas, to avert a looming tragedy—not a Greek tragedy of the theater and mind, but a real and devastating American tragedy, the loss of the greatest republic known to mankind.

TWO

---

# ON THE DEBT

GEORGE MASON UNIVERSITY ECONOMICS professor
Dr. Walter Williams rightly describes the underlying pathol-
ogy driving the nation to economic and financial ruin as a
moral problem: "We've become an immoral people demanding that Congress forcibly use one American to serve the
purposes of another. Deficits and runaway national debt are
merely symptoms of that real problem."[1] As Williams states,
nearly 75 percent of today's federal spending "can be described
as Congress taking the earnings of one American to give to
another through thousands of handout programs, such as farm
subsidies, business bailouts and welfare."[2]

Dr. Thomas Sowell, senior fellow at the Hoover Institute,
Stanford University, notes that "There was a time when the

purpose of taxes was to pay the inevitable costs of government. To the political left, however, taxes have long been seen as a way to redistribute income and finance other social experiments based on liberal ideology."[3]

The consequences for the rising generation and future generations of the statists' immoral, politically expedient, and economically ruinous behavior and policies are unambiguous as evidenced by statistic after statistic, which are mainly ignored, discounted, or excused by most of the media, academia, and, of course, governing statists. Nonetheless, there is no mistaking the eventual societal turmoil these facts and figures portend—evidence all Americans, and especially younger people, must heed.

The nation's fiscal operating debt was already $10.6 trillion on the day President Barack Obama took office in January 2009. By the end of January 2012, however, the fiscal operating debt had increased 44.5 percent to $15.4 trillion. As of April 12, 2015, the fiscal operating debt was $18.152 trillion—a 71 percent increase in less than six and one half years.[4] Each man, woman, and child in this country's share of the national debt has grown from $33,220 at the beginning of the Obama presidency to more than $56,900 today.[5] To be sure, the debt habit began long before the Obama presidency, but it is now a full-blown addiction.

During the Obama administration, government spending and borrowing have both sky-rocketed. The financial bailouts and expanded social spending during the prior administration of George W. Bush contributed mightily to the federal government's debt. In fact, Bush is second only to Obama in the amount of debt in absolute dollars with which he burdened younger people and future generations.[6] But with the addition of the massive Patient Protection and Affordable Care Act program, or Obamacare, and other profligate spending programs, including some $800 billion for the American Recovery and Reinvestment Act of 2009, or "stimulus program," there is no denying that the past several years have created historic records for yearly deficits and overall debt.[7]

As C. Eugene Steuerle of the Urban Institute explained: "Over decades, we have wound [a] straight jacket policy around ourselves. Especially in retirement, health and taxation— budget areas where now-dead or retired members of Congress inscribed permanent policies—annual decision-making and regular review have been choked off and future generations saddled with the tab or forced to raise the resources to meet these past promises."[8]

In July 2014, the nonpartisan Congressional Budget Office (CBO) released its annual Long-Term Budget Outlook. The document provides an extensive analysis of projected government spending, debt, and obligations. It reported that between 2009 and 2012, the federal government amassed the largest budget deficits relative to the size of the economy, the Gross Domestic Product (GDP), since World War II.[9] These deficit levels were almost twice the percentage of the deficit at the end of 2008.[10] Measured in dollars, the federal deficit in 2008 was nearly half a trillion dollars.[11] By 2012, the deficit was $1.4 trillion.[12] In 2014 alone the federal budget deficit was larger than the combined market capitalization of Apple Computers, Exxon Mobil Corporation, and Microsoft—three of the world's largest corporations.[13]

Economists discuss the budget deficit in terms of its percentage of GDP. For most of the forty-plus years before 1998, federal debt held by the public was on average 39 percent of GDP.[14] But when the unprecedented deficits that began at the end of the Bush administration exploded at the beginning of the Obama administration, and swelled further during the course of the Obama administration, the total amount of federal debt held by the public in 2014 rose to nearly 74 percent of GDP. Assuming that current laws remain in place—including the so-called Budget Control Act—federal debt will reach 103 percent of GDP by 2039.[15] CBO's long-term projections do not incorporate the negative economic impacts that are projected to accompany the government's debt burden. When the economic impact is calculated, it is estimated that the debt burden will reach 111 percent of GDP by 2039.[16] "Moreover, debt would be on an upward path relative to the size of the economy, a trend that could not be sustained indefinitely."[17]

Increased public debt also means increased debt-servicing costs, particularly when the Federal Reserve eventually discontinues its artificially low interest rate policy. "When the Fed starts to raise interest rates, rising interest expenses to the Treasury is going to exacerbate the climb in the deficit," according to economist Michael Englund of Action Economics LLC.[18] The increase in interest payments by the federal government will consume a still larger portion of the federal budget, thus increasing the gap between remaining revenues and government benefits and programs.[19] Interest payments are expected to more than double relative to the size of the economy—from 2 percent to 4.5 percent of GDP.[20]

Ever increasing federal spending exacerbates the national debt problem. For most of the past forty years federal spending has averaged 20.5 percent of GDP.[21] But in Obama's first year in office, federal spending spiked to 24.4 percent of GDP—the highest level since World War II.[22] In both 2010 and 2011, expenditures were 23.4 percent of GDP.[23] Even with sequestration cuts and follow-on budget deals, spending was 22 percent of GDP in 2012 and nearly 21 percent of GDP in 2013.[24] CBO projects spending levels to increase to 26 percent of GDP by 2039.[25] This is an immense increase in federal spending. It is attributable to two primary components: federal entitlement spending and debt financing. They are said to be "permanent" fixtures in the budget, which means both are supposedly beyond the reach of Congress's annual budget process.[26]

Social Security and the federal government's health-care programs—Medicare, Medicaid, Children's Health Insurance Program, and subsidies related to Obamacare—will double in relative costs over the next several decades. For the past forty years they have together consumed on average 7 percent of GDP. However, they are expected to increase to 14 percent of GDP by 2039.[27] Social Security, Medicare, and Medicaid account for 60 percent of the government's noninterest expenditures in recent years, steadily growing as a share of annual federal expenditures.[28] For example, in 1970 social programs accounted for 32 percent of total federal expenditures.[29] Social programs grew to 44 percent of federal expenditures in 1980 and 1990, and 54 percent in 2000. They were promoted as safety-net programs for the protection of the poor, elderly, and vulnerable. But in each case the programs have snowballed and have become unsustainable. CBO expects their spending percentages to continue increasing indefinitely.[30] Although this topic will be addressed more fully in a subsequent chapter, suffice it to say that the Social Security benefit cost explosion has been predicted for decades.[31] There are currently 58 million people receiving Social Security benefits. By 2024 that number will grow to about 77 million, and by 2039 there will be 103 million eligible beneficiaries. Average benefits are on the rise as is the number of people qualified to receive benefits. Over the next ten years there will be a 38 percent increase in the number of people over sixty-five years of age and entitled to receive Social Security benefits.[32] By 2039, CBO reports, there will be an 82 percent increase in the number of those who are over sixty-five years of age.

Increases will be caused, in significant part, by the influx of retirees and beneficiaries and the outstretched benefits promised by these programs, particularly with the huge expansion of federal health-care spending.[33] Over the next ten years alone, the percentage of people reaching retirement age will grow from the current 14 percent to 21 percent.[34] Concurrently, the number of income-producing individuals will drop from 60 percent to 54 percent of the population.[35] CBO projects that trend to continue as life expectancy increases.[36] Obviously, that means there will be fewer taxpayers available to pay the freight, a crushing burden imposed on younger people and future generations.

Again, although this will be the subject of a subsequent chapter, it merits mention here that federal spending on health care increased from 9.5 percent of GDP in 1985 to 16.2 percent of GDP in 2012. CBO projects that based on current trends the federal government's health-care expenditures will mushroom to 22 percent of GDP by 2039.[37] In order to pay for these ballooning expenditures, CBO forecasts that payroll taxes will grow significantly over the same time period,[38] yet another enormous weight dropped on the heads of the rising generation.[39]

Not only is federal spending out of control, it is also inefficient and poorly monitored. A recent report issued by the comptroller general of the United States, Gene Dodaro, disclosed that duplicative or overlapping federal spending programs exist in 132 areas, from teacher training to job training.[40] Dodaro also found that improper payments by eighteen different federal departments in 2012 cost the federal government a whopping $107 billion.[41]

In fact, so bad is the federal government's management of its massive resources that the General Accountability Office

(GAO) found the accuracy of most of its financial reporting suspect. In its latest audit of the federal government, the GAO concluded there are significant and material weaknesses in the accounting performed at all levels of the federal government. Among other things, it declared that this incompetence "1) hamper[s] the federal government's ability to reliably report a significant portion of its assets, liabilities, costs, and other related information; 2) affect[s] the federal government's ability to reliably measure the full cost as well as the financial and nonfinancial performance of certain programs and activities; 3) impair[s] the federal government's ability to adequately safeguard significant assets and properly record various transactions; and 4) hinder[s] the federal government from having reliable financial information to operate in an efficient and effective manner. In addition to the three major impediments, GAO identified other material weaknesses. These are the federal government's inability to 1) determine the full extent to which improper payments occur and reasonably assure that appropriate actions are taken to reduce them, 2) identify and resolve information security control deficiencies and manage information security risks on an ongoing basis, and 3) effectively manage its tax collection activities."[42]

In fact, even the GAO and CBO understate the true nature of the economic and financial calamity facing the nation. On February 25, 2015, Boston University professor of economics Dr. Laurence J. Kotlikoff testified before the Senate Budget Committee about "America's fiscal insolvency and its generational consequences." He flatly stated that "Our country is broke. It's not broke in 75 years or 50 years or 25 years or 10 years. It's broke today. Indeed, it may well be in worse fiscal shape than any developed country, including Greece."[43] He condemned Congress for "cooking the books." "Congress's economically arbitrary decisions as to what to put on and what to keep off the books have not been innocent. Successive Congresses, whether dominated by Republicans or Democrats, have spent the postwar accumulating massive net fiscal obligations virtually all of which have been kept off the books."[44] Professor Kotlikoff explained that the real debt picture is far worse than the federal government admits. "The U.S. fiscal gap currently stands at $210 trillion. . . . The size of the U.S. fiscal gap—$210 trillion—is massive. It's 16 times larger than official U.S. debt, which indicates precisely how useless official debt is for understanding our nation's true fiscal position."[45] "In 2013 the fiscal gap stood at $205 trillion. In 2014 it was $210 trillion. Hence, the country's true 2014 deficit—the increase in its fiscal gap—was $5 trillion, not the $483 billion increase in official debt reported by the CBO."[46]

Professor Kotlikoff concluded what should be obvious to all: "U.S. postwar generational policy is accurately characterized as 'Take As You Go.' Over the decades Republican and Democratic Congresses and Administrations have taken ever-larger amounts of resources from young workers and transferred them to old retirees. The resources taken from the young and given to the old were called, in the main, 'taxes.' And the

young were effectively told, 'Don't worry. We are calling these
resources taxes, but when you are old, you will receive massive
transfer payments that more than make up for what you are
paying now.'"[47] Thus, there is a colossal transfer of wealth not
yet created, by younger people and future generations, to the
governing generation and generations since passed, which will
doom America's children and grandchildren if left unabated.

Moreover, the nation's increasing debt burden will wreak
havoc on the economy in very specific ways—higher interest rates, slower economic growth, weaker job markets, higher
taxes, and higher inflation rates.[48] The CBO notes that the
enormous amount of government securities required to finance
debt crowd out investments by individuals and businesses in
the private marketplace, including in manufacturing, research,
infrastructure, and small and large business opportunities.[49]
"Because wages are determined mainly by workers' productivity, the reduction in investment would reduce wages as well,
lessening people's incentive to work."[50] In order to compete
for investments, both government and private borrowers will
face higher interest rates.[51] While those rising interest rates
will encourage individuals to save, the offsetting growth in
interest costs will increase the cost of borrowing, thus further
driving up the cost of the debt.[52]

The late Dr. Edward M. Gramlich, former Federal Reserve Board governor, explained that "For workers to become
more productive, investments must be made in education and
training; in modernized plants, equipment, and productive

techniques; in new discoveries and innovations; and in transportation, communications, and other infrastructure. To make these investments, there must be a pool of savings that can be used for this purpose. Historically, the United States has had a particularly low rate of private savings, but, what is worse; the federal government's deficit is financed by soaking up much of the savings we do manage to put away. When the government spends more money than it has, it borrows the rest. Most of the money borrowed comes from private savings."[53]

Dr. Gramlich went on to warn that we cannot ignore the consequences of deficits much longer because they will lead to a stagnant long-term economy that will not only be unable to support Social Security, Medicare, and other social programs, but will not be able to provide opportunity for today's youth who will be paying the bills.[54]

Professor Kotlikoff also points out that the impact of these policies has had another predictable outcome: "Older generations consumed more, younger generations had no or little reason to consume less, and the national saving rate fell."[55]

A Moody's Analytics analysis shows that workers under the age of thirty-five have gone from saving a small percentage of their incomes shortly after the 2009 recession to a current savings rate of negative 2 percent.[56] In 2009, the savings rate for younger people was over 5 percent.[57] A good rule of thumb is that a healthy savings rate is around 10 percent.[58] Consequently, the very low savings rate among younger people is a sobering indicator of financial precariousness.

Debt accumulation—especially student loan and credit card debt—is a major contributor to the problem.[59] Forty million Americans now have at least one student loan and in most cases at least four student loans to repay.[60] Just six years ago, only 29 million Americans carried student loan debt.[61] The average balance on these loans has also increased from $25,000 to $29,000 since 2008.[62] Moreover, "[s]tudent loan debt has tripled from a decade earlier, to more than $1 trillion, while wages for young college graduates have dropped."[63] Fully 55 percent of those members of the rising generation with student loans are concerned that they may not be able to pay off their debt.[64] And an alarming 43 percent have used nontraditional, high-cost forms of borrowing such as payday loans, pawn shops, and auto title loans.[65]

High credit card debt is another indicator of financial instability. Prior generations tended to incur credit card debt in their youth and pay it off once careers were established in middle age.[66] But now, according to Ohio State University economics professor Lucia Dunn, "Millennials are not only going deeper into debt than earlier generations did at the same age, they are paying it off so much more slowly that they will die still owing money."[67] The tendency to make only minimum payments on their credit card balances suggest credit card debt for younger people will continue to grow well into their seventies.[68]

Many younger people have to delay major purchases of homes and automobiles; money is being diverted from retirement accounts; there are fewer business start-ups; and families are being delayed.[69] Mark Zandi, chief economist at Moody's Analytics, points out that over time the consequences are severe. "It's not one of those things that matters a lot in a given year, but over a couple decades or generation or two, it matters a great deal."[70]

According to a recent Pew Research study, younger people aged eighteen to thirty-two years old "are the first in the modern era to have higher levels of student loan debt, poverty, and unemployment and lower levels of wealth and personal income than their two immediate predecessor generations had at the same age."[71] The Census Bureau reports, in part, that "One in five young adults [eighteen to thirty-four years old] lives in poverty (13.5 million people), up from one in seven (8.4 million people) in 1980 and . . . 65 percent of young adults are employed, down from 69 percent in 1980."[72] What is more, in 1980, 22.9 percent of young adults were living with a parent deemed the householder; in 1990, the percentage increased to 24.2 percent; in 2000, the number dropped to 23.2 percent; but in 2009–2013, a record 30.3 percent were living at home with a parent.[73]

When confronted with this debt debacle, the statists' usual and deceitful bromide is a demagogic appeal to income redistribution—that is, to demand higher taxes on "the rich" or a "more progressive" income tax where "everyone pays their fair share." The fact is that if the federal government confiscated every penny produced by the private economy for the next decade, assuming a yearly average GDP of $20 trillion

(today, it is $17.4 trillion annually[74]), in the eleventh year
the aggregate national debt would still amount to trillions of
dollars. In addition, the federal government's own statistics, as
analyzed by the nonpartisan Tax Policy Center, belie the class
warfare, redistributionist agitprop. In the 2014 tax year, the
top 20 percent of earners paid 84 percent of individual federal
income taxes. Indeed, the top 1 percent of earners paid nearly
half of the federal income tax. The bottom 40 percent of earners paid no federal income taxes. Even more, they receive federal government subsidies, including the Earned Income Tax
Credit, amounting to tens of billions of dollars.[75]

Ultimately this is not merely about dreary yet didactic
statistics but, as Dr. Williams insisted, it is about morality.
The devastating consequences of wealth redistribution, intergenerational thievery, massive federal spending, endless borrowing, and unimaginable debt accumulation on American
society, and most particularly on the ruling generation and
future generations, are a travesty. Stealing from the future does
not establish the utopia promised by the statists. It is the rising
generation's grave moral failure.

In his farewell address to the nation after serving two terms
as president, George Washington urged his fellow citizens to
"avoid . . . the accumulation of debt not only by shunning oc-
casions of expense but by vigorous exertions to discharge the
debts, not throwing upon posterity the burden which we ourselves ought to bear."[76]

THREE

_____

ON SOCIAL SECURITY

THE LARGEST SINGLE COMPONENT of the federal budget, and perhaps the greatest and most financially devastating burden imposed on younger people and future generations, is the Social Security program. This is not a recent development. Since 1993, it has outspent defense appropriations. As a percentage of federal spending, Social Security's expenditures have ranged from 0.22 percent during World War II to 24 percent in 2013.[1] And Social Security costs are actually skyrocketing.

Social Security has expanded from its original scope in 1935 to include workers' dependents and survivors as well as the disabled. As a result, there are roughly 58 million people receiving benefits—more than double the number in 1970.[2]

As members of the ruling generation begin to retire, many more will be eligible for benefits. Unfortunately, there will not be nearly enough younger people working to pay the current rate of taxes to subsidize them. In 1940, there were 159 workers for every beneficiary. That ratio has dropped precipitously, from 16.5 in 1950, to 5.1 in 1960, to 3.7 in 1970 to slightly below 3 in 2010—and it is projected to get worse.[3] There will only be 2.2 workers for every beneficiary in 2030.[4]

Social Security provides benefits through two major programs—Old Age and Survivors Insurance (OASI) and Disability Insurance (DI).[5] Note the use of the word "insurance." It is a fiction, about which I will elaborate later. The OASI program provides payments to retirees and, in certain circumstances, to their dependents; DI provides payments to people who are disabled and presumably cannot work. OASI and DI have separate "trust funds." But for simplicity's sake they are usually considered together when their financial viability is analyzed.

Theoretically, Social Security is financed by payroll taxes on employees and employers and, to a lesser extent, taxes on Social Security benefits and income from trust fund assets. FICA taxes—payroll taxes under the Federal Insurance Contributions Act—are falsely said to fund Social Security and part of Medicare. Payroll taxes, as opposed to income taxes, apply to employees regardless of their income. They are most onerous on poorer workers and, of course, younger people who are just entering the workplace. They are also effectively a tax on employment as the employer must consider this fixed additional cost in his hiring decisions.

The rate of taxation to supposedly "fund" Social Security has been increasing over time. Currently workers pay 6.2 percent of their first $117,000 of earnings in Social Security taxes and their employers pay an additional 6.2 percent. The self-employed pay the full 12.4 percent themselves.[6] When the program started in the 1930s, however, the tax rate was only 1 percent of income on a much lower income threshold and did not reach 3 percent until 1960.[7] In fact, the amount of money subject to the Social Security payroll tax has grown significantly over time. From the 1930s until 1950, workers paid tax on the first $3,000 of their income. That cap did not reach $10,000 until the 1970s. Presently, workers pay FICA taxes on the first $117,000 of their income, and that amount will continue to rise with increases in the average wage.[8]

The age when retirement benefits are available has also increased. Initially, individuals had to live to age 65 to receive full benefits, with a reduced benefit for early retirement available at age 62. Today the full benefit age is 66 for individuals born in 1943–1954, and it is slated to go to 67 for individuals born in 1960 or later. Early retirement benefits will still be available at 62 years of age but at a reduced level. In 1984, recipients were required to pay income taxes on up to 50 percent of their benefits if their total income met a certain threshold of adjusted gross income. In 1993, even more of those benefits became subject to taxation and at a higher rate.[9] In short, to-

day's workers are paying a higher tax rate on a larger portion of
their income than many of the retirees whom they are helping
to subsidize. They are also required to wait until they are older
to receive benefits and will pay income taxes on a portion of
those benefits.

But here is the worst news for younger workers and future
generations. According to the Associated Press, a "historic
shift" is occurring:

> If you retired in 1960, you could expect to get back seven
> times more in benefits than you paid in Social Security
> taxes, and more if you were a low-income worker, as long
> as you made it to age 78 for men and 81 for women. As
> recently as 1985, workers at every income level could re-
> tire and expect to get more in benefits than they paid in
> Social Security taxes, though they didn't do quite as well
> as their parents and grandparents. Not anymore.[10]

For the first time, people who are retiring today will receive less in benefits than they paid into the system in taxes.
A lot of factors are involved in making these comparisons, of
course, such as how long someone lives after retirement, how
much they earned and thus paid into "the system," when they
decided to start receiving benefits, and so forth. (Incidentally,
Social Security itself is very complicated. The Social Security Handbook "has 2,728 separate rules governing its benefits. And it has thousands upon thousands of explanations
of those rules in its Program Operating Manual System.")[11]

But in 2011, the Urban Institute found that a married couple who earned average lifetime salaries retiring that year had paid about $598,000 in Social Security taxes during their working years. However, they can only expect to receive about $556,000 in lifetime retirement benefits, assuming the husband lives to eighty-two and the wife lives to eighty-five.[12]

Nonetheless, Social Security is simultaneously growing and losing money. And these losses will become increasingly severe. In 2010, more money went to subsidize benefits than were received from taxes. According to the trustees of the Social Security "trust funds," there will be a cash deficit averaging about $77 billion annually through 2018, which will then rise steeply as the number of beneficiaries continues to grow at a substantially faster rate than the number of covered workers.[13] The ratio of beneficiaries to workers that I described earlier gets much worse. The combined DI and OASI "trust funds" will be completely depleted by 2033.[14] In fact, the trustees forecast that expenditures will exceed tax revenues throughout the next seventy-five years.[15] When they calculate the present value of the unfunded obligation for the next seventy-five years, it comes to $10.6 trillion, or $1 trillion more than last year's prediction.[16] Indeed, the $10.6 trillion will be necessary to fund obligations *on top of* the income the federal government receives from Social Security taxes.

The future suggests several unpleasant scenarios. Benefits will be slashed, benefits or other income will be heavily taxed, the retirement age will be pushed back further, and/or the federal government will eliminate other spending or go further into debt. Inasmuch as those retiring today will receive less than they "contributed" over the years into the system, it is difficult to see how younger people will be left with anything but horrendous debt and broken promises.

The late writer and economist Henry Hazlitt argued that this phenomenon is part of a broader problem. He explained that there are two factors that give rise to the majority of mistakes in economic policy: the "special pleading of selfish interests" and the tendency to ignore secondary consequences.[17] The first factor is clear. Some economic policies benefit everyone or nearly everyone, while other policies only benefit a distinct group to the detriment of everyone else. For example, consider a proposal to subsidize corn producers. The group directly benefiting from the policy, in this case corn farmers, will vigorously lobby Congress for the subsidy. Members of Congress will get letters, visits, and contributions from farmers and their trade associations. However, they will hear almost nothing from the public at large on such a narrow issue. Therefore, the interests of the vocal minority will receive more weight than the interests of the majority. The measure passes as part of an omnibus spending bill and the cost of the new subsidy is added to the trillions of dollars spent every year by the federal government. The same has held true for Social Security over the years. Organized and vocal groups claiming to represent retirees and the soon to retire have successfully lobbied lawmakers to increase the number of individuals qualifying for Social Security and the amount and variety of benefits.

The second factor describes the tendency for public policy to be based on its immediate effects or its effect on a specific group without regard to long-term consequences for the economy and nation generally. For example, the benefits of a taxpayer bailout to a failing carmaker are immediate and evident for the carmaker, its investors, and its employees. But the financial dislocation and lost fiscal opportunities resulting from the diversion of economic resources to tax subsidies are distant and disregarded. If the carmaker files for bankruptcy, the company is able and required to streamline its operations, including reducing its workforce and employee benefits and offloading certain debt. Although this allows the newly organized company a fresh opportunity to regain profitability and survive in the longer term, including expanding and hiring down the road, the immediate upshot of the reorganization, with its downsizing, and so on, is visible and tangible. Hazlitt explained the phenomenon this way:

In this lies almost the whole difference between good economics and bad. The bad economist sees only what immediately strikes the eye; the good economist also looks beyond. The bad economist sees only the direct consequences of a proposed course; the good economist looks also at the longer and indirect consequences. The

bad economist sees only what the effect of a given policy
has been or will be on one particular group; the good
economist inquires also what the effect of the policy will
be on all groups.[18]


Clearly the ruling generation and generations unborn are
harmed most by these practices, particularly with massive generational transfer payments and debt accumulation. Younger
people do not have powerful organizations lobbying the federal government on their behalf against current and future
profligate spending and borrowing. Conversely, the American Association of Retired People (AARP) is an extremely
powerful and influential presence on Capitol Hill, relentlessly
pressuring Congress for expanded government subsidies for the
rising generation and against most serious efforts to reform Social Security and Medicare.

At the heart of the problem is the ruse that Social Security is an insurance program, making an honest national
discussion about it extremely difficult. In truth, in no legal,
ethical, or rational sense are there actually trust funds or individual trust accounts. Most workers pay into the system each
month or bimonthly. In turn, those tax proceeds are used to
pay *current* Social Security beneficiaries. Therefore, it differs
fundamentally from an individual, directly funded insurance
policy or pension fund account like a 401(k), where a person
contributes to a specific account over time and that money is

invested just for the beneficiary's future. In fact, Social Security is not even a true pay-as-you-go system. In the past, when more money was received by the federal government than was necessary to cover current beneficiaries, the excess funds were not returned to the taxpayers. Instead, the taxes were used to fund other general expenditures of the federal government. Of course, this is a shell game. If any private investment firm or insurance company conducted itself this way, it would risk prosecution for conducting an unlawful Ponzi scheme. And today, younger workers are compelled to "contribute" payroll taxes into a system that benefits current retirees and will not exist, at least not as promised, when they reach retirement age.

Consequently, there are no real assets in the Social Security "trust funds." The federal government uses an accounting measure reflecting how one part of the government owes money to another. At best it can be said that Social Security "trust funds" consist of specially issued government bonds that earn interest. Even so, the interest is owed by the federal government, requiring it to issue additional IOUs to the Treasury Department. Presumably, when the federal government runs out of funds to pay Social Security benefits, it will have to cash in those bonds. But from where does the money to pay off the bonds come? The general revenue of the federal government—that is, the taxpayers and the accumulation of more debt. The late Nobel Laureate for Economics, Dr. Milton Friedman, explained that these "trust funds" are nothing but

an accounting measure to mislead the public and "preserve the
fiction that Social Security is insurance."[19]

Dr. Friedman described how Social Security uses terms like
"contributions" and "benefits" instead of "taxes" and "subsidies." The statists use these terms and others, such as "Old
Age and Survivors Insurance," intentionally. In point of fact,
after Social Security was enacted as part of President Franklin Roosevelt's New Deal, he acknowledged to an aide that
the payroll taxes used to "fund" the system were regressive,
but their purpose was actually political. Roosevelt declared: "I
guess you're right on the economics. They are politics all the
way through. We put those payroll contributions there so as
to give the contributors a legal, moral, and political right to
collect their pensions and their unemployment benefits. With
those taxes in there, no damn politician can ever scrap my
social security program."[20] As I pointed out in *Liberty and Tyranny*, "The taxes may never have been a problem of economics to Roosevelt, but the economic problem he unleashed on
American society has become immense, thanks to the politics
he played with the people and their future."[21]

It is both unnerving and unsurprising how little knowledge
the New Deal masterminds possessed when remaking the federal government. Remarkably, the age originally established
for the receipt of full Social Security benefits was not based
on a thorough analysis, despite that single decision's effect on
the economy, the size of the workforce, tax revenues, savings
rates, and so on. Instead, it was literally plucked from thin air.

Why was age 65 chosen . . . ? According to Robert Myers, who worked on the creation of the Social Security program beginning in 1934 and later served in various senior and appointed capacities at the Social Security Administration, "why not?" Myers wrote, "Age 65 was picked because 60 was too young and 70 was too old. So we split the difference."[22]

Moreover, when Roosevelt signed the Social Security Act in 1935, he boldly proclaimed his utopian ambition thusly:

This law . . . represents a cornerstone in a structure which is being built but is by no means complete. It is a structure intended to lessen the force of possible future depressions. *It will act as a protection to future Administrations against the necessity of going deeply into debt to furnish relief to the needy.* The law will flatten out the peaks and valleys of deflation and of inflation. It is, in short, a law that will take care of human needs and at the same time provide for the United States an economic structure of vastly greater soundness.[23] (Italics added)

Of course, many have benefited from Social Security over the decades, especially the elderly. But the overall structure, which as Roosevelt insisted at the outset, put politics before economics, was and is, in the end, economically and fiscally irrational and irresponsible. Recently, another warning was issued by the Congressional Budget Office (CBO) in its 2014 annual budget outlook, in which it announced that Social Security (and other entitlement programs) is "unsustainable" and will drive federally held debt to historic levels, thereby threatening the overall economy.[24]

Top elected officeholders in the nation have been repeatedly and specifically warned about the coming upheaval. As compelled by law, on July 28, 2014, Social Security's trustees issued their annual letters to both House Speaker John Boehner and Senate President (Vice President) Joe Biden on the financial state of, among other things, the Social Security system. They wrote, in part: "Estimates in the 2014 Trustees Report show that although the Old-Age and Survivors Insurance (OASI) Trust Fund and the theoretical combined OASI and Disability Insurance (DI) Trust Funds are adequately financed . . . through the next 10 years under intermediate assumptions, the DI fund alone is not. Under the intermediate assumptions of the 2014 Trustees Report (those representing the Trustees' best estimate of future economic and demographic trends), the DI Trust Fund reserves steadily decline, falling below 20 percent of annual cost by the beginning of calendar year 2016 and becoming *depleted in the fourth calendar quarter of 2016*."[25] (Italics added) If anything, the trustees understate the overall and looming Social Security disaster.

Predictably, the statists cling zealously to their utopianism and dogmatically reject virtually every suggestion to restructure Social Security. On October 15, 2010, 101 Democratic members of Congress wrote President Obama, insisting that any proposals by the National Commission on Fiscal Responsibility and Reform to modify Social Security benefits, adjust age requirements, or introduce private investment options would be blocked in Congress. They declared, in part: "We write today to express our strong support for Social Security and our view that it should be strengthened. We oppose any cuts to Social Security benefits, including raising the retirement age. We also oppose any effort to privatize Social Security, in whole or in part. . . . If any of the Commission's recommendations cut or diminish Social Security in any way, we will stand firmly against them."[26]

Rather than exploring even modest but still meaningful options and alternatives to the current "unsustainable" Social Security system—such as ensuring that workers age fifty-five and over remain covered under the traditional Social Security system with no change in promised benefits, while allowing younger workers to opt out of Social Security and invest in private sector retirement alternatives—statists demand greater federal centralization and control, this time over the individual's *private* retirement plans, as an increasingly desperate federal government looks for ways to expand its reach and confiscate more earnings from the rising generation.

For example, 401(k) plans have enabled approximately 52 million American workers to own stocks and bonds as part of their private retirement portfolios. But there is a growing movement to eliminate these tax and savings benefits in order to further fund federal "insurance." As explained by the Cato

Institute's Michael D. Tanner: "Teresa Ghilarducci, director of
the Schwartz Center for Economic Policy Analysis at the New
School in New York, has argued before Congress that 401(k)
plans should be abolished, and replaced by an expanded social-
insurance system. Representative Jim McDermott (D., Wash.),
who sits on the tax-writing Ways and Means Committee, has
pronounced himself 'intrigued' by Ghilarducci's ideas. And
[former] Congressman George Miller (D., Calif.) has called for
eliminating or reducing the tax break for 401(k) contributions.
The Obama administration has also sought to limit tax breaks
for 401(k)s, although primarily for wealthier participants. In
a speech calling for the expansion of Social Security, Senator
Elizabeth Warren (D., Mass.) criticized private retirement accounts like 401(k) plans 'that leave the retiree at the mercy
of a market that rises and falls, and, sometimes, at the mercy
of dangerous investment products.'" Tanner points out that
"No policy proposed in recent years would have done more to
expand capital ownership than allowing younger workers to
invest a portion of their Social Security taxes through personal
accounts. One of the unsung benefits of such Social Security
reform is that it would enable even the lowest-paid American
worker to benefit from capital investment. Indeed, since the
wealthy presumably already invest as much as they wish to,
lower-income workers would be the primary beneficiaries of
this new investment opportunity."[27]

The American people are facing some very unpleasant realities about the nation's financial vulnerabilities. The federal

government is deeply in debt; the largest federal program, Social Security, is hemorrhaging money; the national birthrate does not provide enough working people from whom money can be transferred to subsidize beneficiaries; and most individuals do not have enough personal savings to get them through severe economic times. As the late economist Dr. Herbert Stein once wrote, "If something can't go on forever, it will stop."[28] And in this case, the federal government's biggest program will stop with a crash, taking down the older recipients and the younger payers alike.

FOUR

---

# ON MEDICARE AND OBAMACARE

ANOTHER IMPENDING FIASCO FOR America's younger people and future generations involves the federal government's control over health care. In the United States, trillions of dollars are spent each year on health care. The Centers for Medicare and Medicaid Services (CMS), a federal agency within the Department of Health and Human Services (HHS), estimated that national health expenditures were $2.8 trillion in 2012, or about 17.2 percent of America's Gross Domestic Product (GDP).[1] Others have noted that there are hundreds of billions in hidden costs that should be added to that number, such as costs to families who serve as home caregivers and money spent on vitamins, bringing the total to over $3 trillion annually.[2]

But the amount spent on health care is not, by itself, the key. North Korea's tyrannical regime spends a lot less per person on health care than the United States and no one in his right mind would advocate switching systems. Similarly, Bangladesh, also among the world's poorest nations, spends a far lower percentage of GDP on health care, a mere 3.6 percent.[3] Most Americans would agree that there are few human and moral priorities more important than the mental and physical health of an individual or family. The key problem in America is the increasingly centralized role of government in the provision of health-care services, which does, in fact, become administratively unmanageable and financially unsustainable over time. Top-down command-and-control decision-making, combined with political and social engineering and redistributive subsidies, destroy the application of genuine insurance practices; distort and eventually contract the marketplace; hugely inflate costs; generate widespread economic inefficiencies, unpredictability, and scarcity; and, severely diminish the quality of health-care services and their availability to countless patients.

The federal government provides health insurance, funds to state health-care programs, or direct care to the elderly (Medicare), the poor (Medicaid), the children of those not poor enough for Medicaid (Children's Health Insurance Program or CHIP), the military (TRICARE), and veterans (the Veterans Administration). The largest of the programs, Medicare, provides health-care coverage to nearly all seniors over the age of sixty-five. In 2014, about 54 million individuals were eligible for Medicare (45 million seniors and 9 million disabled individuals) for a total cost of $612 billion.[4] As with Social Security, the scope of covered individuals and services has grown significantly since Medicare's inception in 1965. And like Social Security, it has required ever greater federal taxes and subsidies to support it. Meanwhile, the number of individuals retiring and becoming eligible for Medicare is soaring. Once again, the ratio of younger workers to older beneficiaries is declining. Moreover, Medicare's financial condition is even worse than Social Security's, as its expenses are growing at a faster rate. Nonetheless, in 2010 the federal government's role in health care hugely expanded in depth and scope with the adoption of the mammoth Patient Protection and Affordable Care Act, or Obamacare. One indication of the size of this new program is that the original statute was well over two thousand pages in length. By 2013, tens of thousands of pages of related regulations were issued, totaling almost 11,600,000 words.[5]

The time is not far off when federal health-care programs, combined with Social Security, will actually consume the vast majority of the federal budget, leaving little room for much else. In fiscal year 2013, 41 percent of the federal government's expenditures supported just Social Security and Medicare.[6] The Congressional Budget Office's (CBO's) long-term budget projections, using a baseline of current spending, concludes that by 2039 federal spending for Social Security and the country's major health-care programs (Medicare, Medicaid, the Children's Health Insurance Program, and Obamacare) will grow to 14 percent of GDP. That is twice the average over the past forty years.[7]

In addition, state budgets are now swamped by health-care spending, in particular Medicaid. Medicaid consumes almost 26 percent of total state expenditures. It is administered by the states with partial financial support from the federal government.[8] One of the major provisions of Obamacare was an expansion of Medicaid, in which states were enticed with initial federal subsidies to cover even more individuals. Though Medicaid was once considered a program solely for the poor, the eligibility requirements were loosened to cover those making 138 percent of the poverty line—that is, an annual income of $16,105 for an individual and $32,913 for a family of four.[9] Since the expansion went into effect, 9.1 million people have been added to Medicaid.[10] In return for covering more people, the federal government agreed to pay the states 100 percent of the additional costs for the first three years, which decreases to 90 percent by 2020.[11] Thereafter, which level of government is responsible for funding and for how much cannot be known. However, already Medicaid enrollment and spending under Obamacare are soaring.[12] But in the end, younger people and future generations will bear the brunt of the financial hardship.

Again, the CBO has declared that the size and growth of the federal debt, most of which is owing to unfunded entitlement liabilities—especially Medicare and Social Security—is a threat to the future viability of the nation. "The large amount of federal borrowing would draw money away from private investment in productive capital in the long term, because the portion of people's savings used to buy government securities would not be available to finance private investment. The result would be a smaller stock of capital and lower output and income than would otherwise be the case, all else being equal . . . ; [f]ederal spending on interest payments would rise, thus requiring higher taxes, lower spending for benefits and services, or both to achieve any chosen targets for budget deficits and debt; [t]he large amount of debt would restrict policymakers' ability to use tax and spending policies to respond to unexpected challenges, such as economic downturns or financial crises."[13] "As a result, those challenges would tend to have larger negative effects on the economy and on people's well-being than they would otherwise. The large amount of debt could also compromise national security by constraining defense spending in times of international crisis or by limiting the country's ability to prepare for such a crisis."[14]

As many younger people have no idea how Medicare works and do not have much interest in the subject, despite its ominous drag on their future, a short tutorial may be useful.

Medicare was signed into law in 1965 by President Lyndon Johnson. He described it as another insurance system: "[T]hrough this new law . . . every citizen will be able, in his productive years when he is earning, to insure himself against the ravages of illness in his old age."[15] Today Medicare is administered by the Centers for Medicare and Medicaid Services (CMS). It originally worked through two components: Part A, Hospital Insurance (HI), which covers costs associated with stays at hospitals, hospices, and nursing facilities; and Part B, Supplementary Medical Insurance (SMI), which covers doctors, outpatient treatment, and durable equipment.

In 1997, Congress and President Bill Clinton expanded Medicare coverage to include Part C, Medicare Advantage (MA), which set up a system allowing the selection of health insurance through private companies, which, in turn, are subsidized by the federal government. (Most participants choose Parts A and B.) In 2003, Congress and President George W. Bush again expanded Medicare coverage to include Part D, prescription drug plans.

Part A automatically covers an individual based on age or disability. Like Social Security, Part A HI is in theory financed primarily through the Federal Insurance Contributions Act (FICA) payroll taxes on employees and employers. Employees pay 1.45 percent of their earnings, which is matched by the employer, and the self-employed pay the full 2.9 percent. This rate used to have the same cap on income as Social Security, but the cap was completely removed in 1990. When the program started, the tax rate was only .35 percent on the first $6,600 of income, the same tax base as Social Security. Johnson claimed that the average worker would pay about $1.50 a month for hospital insurance protection in the program's

PLUNDER AND DECEIT          59

first year.[16] Within six years, however, the rate jumped from
.35 percent to 1 percent a year, a 185 percent increase.

By contrast, Part B is voluntary. It is said to be a form of
insurance, although it actually does not function that way, but
it does require the payment of premiums and copays. In 1966,
the premium was set at $3.00 a month. Each year the pre-
mium changes, and the premiums are also adjusted according
to certain income levels. The Congressional Research Service
(CRS) reports: "The standard monthly Part B premium for
2014 is $104.90. Higher-income beneficiaries, currently de-
fined as those with incomes over $85,000 a year, or couples
with incomes over $170,000 per year, pay $146.90, $209.80,
$272.70, or $335.70 per month, depending on their income
levels."[17] Part D, the prescription drug program, is also voluntary and is funded mostly by premiums and general tax
revenues. As with Part B, it initially provided for a uniform
premium, but now the formula includes higher premiums on
higher earners.

The history of Medicare is similar to that of Social Security. It was first touted as an insurance system, but it never was.
And it has grown into a centralized, bureaucratic octopus with
tentacles reaching in every direction.

One thing is clear: Younger people are taxed today for
promises of comprehensive health-care coverage in their senior years, which is simply impossible. Over the longer run,
the Medicare design was political in nature and could never

work as a rational economic model. Like Social Security, today
it is simultaneously expanding and imploding.

Of course, those who have already retired have benefited
considerably from the system. The evidence demonstrates
that an average worker who retired in 2011 would have paid
$60,000 in Medicare-related taxes yet received $170,000 in
benefits.[18] This system cannot last forever, and it will not,
given reality and mathematics. Indeed, in 2014, the trustees
overseeing Medicare declared that the HI trust fund will run
dry in 2030.[19] The trustees also predict that Medicare will take
an even larger share of the nation's resources, nearly doubling
from 3.5 percent of GDP in 2013 to 6.9 percent in 2088.[20] In
fact, the present value of the HI trust fund's unfunded obliga-
tion through 2075 is $3.6 trillion.[21] Consequently, not only
will future generations lose the tax "contributions" they have
"paid into Medicare trust funds," for they will no longer exist
even in theory, but they will have to bear the impossible burden of Medicare's massive unfunded obligations.

In addition, Medicare has a perverse effect on the delivery of quality health-care services, which will only exacerbate
over time. For example, obviously the health-care system cannot function well without the services of doctors and other
providers. Doctors are largely paid on a "fee for service" basis.
Initially, Medicare reimbursed doctors for "usual, customary
and reasonable" fees. Such a vague standard paid by a distant third party was soon blamed for rising costs. Therefore,
about twenty-five years ago, the federal government created

an incredibly complex standardized payment scheme—the Resource-Based Relative Value Scale (RBRVS). This system sought to assign a numerical value to the multitude of medical services. As described by the American Medical Association (AMA): "In the RBRVS system, payments for services are determined by the resource costs needed to provide them. The cost of providing each service is divided into three components: physician work, practice expense and professional liability insurance. Payments are calculated by multiplying the combined costs of a service by a conversion factor (a monetary amount that is determined by the Centers for Medicare and Medicaid Services). Payments are also adjusted for geographical differences in resource costs."[22]

The RBRVS system assigns a relative value to a given procedure. The values are updated periodically by a handful of individuals from the AMA who serve on the Relative Value Update Committee (RUC). They meet in secret each year to discuss and reach their decisions. The federal government adopts nearly all of the RUC's recommendations. The effects of this centralized, byzantine approach and point system are not limited to Medicare because of Medicare's size and influence over the entire health-care system—roughly 80 percent of private insurers use the point system for their own payment structures.[23] Therefore, the impracticability of Medicare's centralized management and archaic decision-making practices also significantly impairs the broader private sector.

The absurdity of the federal government's top-down control over health care is perhaps best explained with a simple example. The retail price for a loaf of bread is different in New York than it is in Alabama. There are differences in price for a loaf of bread between towns and cities in the same state—such as Brooklyn, New York, and Utica, New York. The reason is there are untold factors relating to resources, allocation, labor, administration, and so on, which go into the cost of planting, harvesting, transporting, processing, baking, packaging, labeling, and transporting again a loaf of bread, as with any product. There are also countless regulations and taxes at every level of the process, from beginning to end, and they differ from jurisdiction to jurisdiction.

Imagine the disorder and dislocation, including cost increases, supply shortages, and instability, if the federal government were in charge of supervising the production and delivery of a loaf of bread. It has been tried by many totalitarian regimes with terrible consequences. Yet the health-care system, which the federal government increasingly monopolizes, is far more complicated and intricate than the numerous processes involved in putting bread on the family table.

Unsurprisingly, another outcome from government's omnipresence in the health-care system is vast levels of fraud, waste, and abuse. On June 25, 2014, the General Accountability Office (GAO) reported: "We have designated Medicare as a high-risk program since 1990, in part because we found the program's size and complexity make it vulnerable to fraud, waste, and abuse. Although there have been convictions for

PLUNDER AND DECEIT 63

multimillion-dollar schemes that defrauded the Medicare program, the extent of the problem is unknown. There are no reliable estimates of the extent of fraud in the Medicare program or for the health care industry as a whole. By its very nature, fraud is difficult to detect, as those involved are engaged in intentional deception."[24]

Nonetheless, the GAO pointed out that in 2013 "The Centers for Medicare & Medicaid Services . . . estimated that improper payments in the Medicare program were almost $50 billion in fiscal year 2013, about $5 billion higher than in 2012. Improper payments may be a result of fraud, waste, or abuse, but it is important to distinguish that the $50 billion in estimated improper payments reported by CMS in fiscal year 2013 is not an estimate of fraud in Medicare. Reported improper payment estimates include many types of payments that should not have been made or were made in an incorrect amount such as overpayments, underpayments, and payments that were not adequately documented."[25]

Sadly, there is more. There exists another layer of complexity that is bewildering to patients and adds heavy administrative costs to health-care providers: medical codes. The AMA developed Current Procedural Technology (CPT) codes in the 1960s, which assign a number for every service a doctor or facility provides as a way to introduce uniformity in medical records. There are thousands of such codes, which are updated each year. Now these codes have spawned more codes. In 1983, CMS incorporated CPT codes into the billing process for Medicare through the development of the Health-care Common Procedure Coding System (HCPCS).[26] HCPCS codes include CPT codes for services as well as codes for supplies, devices, and equipment provided to patients. There is also an outpatient code system for diagnoses and disorders—International Classification of Diseases, 9th revision, Clinical Modification or ICD-9-CM codes. Health-care providers are required to use all these codes on claims for reimbursement from Medicare and private insurers.

As the consolidation of health-care management tightens further, the federal government is about to require a switch from ICD-9, which has 13,000 codes, to ICD-10, which has 68,000 codes.[27] In the new system, there are separate codes for injuries sustained while "sewing, ironing, playing a brass instrument, crocheting, doing handicrafts, or knitting" or injuries caused by a bird, duck, macaw, parrot, goose, or turkey.[28] Tracking existing injuries will also require more intricate codes: "the one code for suturing an artery will become 195 codes, designating every single artery, among other variables."[29]

This unfathomable coding system, which engulfs doctors' offices in suffocating administrative minutiae unrelated to the provision of timely and quality medical services, is also prone to error and outright fraud. In May 2014, the Office of the Inspector General (IG) for the HHS conducted a review of doctors' reimbursement claims for office visits and other evaluations (E/M services) for calendar year 2010. It discovered that

"Medicare inappropriately paid $6.7 billion for claims for E/M services in 2010 that were incorrectly coded and/or lacking documentation."[30] These payments accounted for 21 percent of Medicare payments for this type of visit for the year. The IG also discovered that 42 percent of claims for such services in 2010 were incorrectly coded—billing too much or too little—and 19 percent lacked documentation.[31]

Despite the backdrop of spiraling costs, centralized decision-making, administrative overkill, and widespread waste, fraud, and abuse, in 2010 a Democratic Congress passed, and Obama signed, the most dramatic expansion of federal control over health care since the passage of Medicare and Medicaid nearly fifty years earlier—Obamacare.

For starters, the Heritage Foundation estimates that by 2023, Obamacare will add $1.8 trillion to federal health-care spending.[32] It also requires individuals to purchase insurance policies (whether they want to or not) and moves other people onto the Medicaid rolls by loosening eligibility requirements and subsidizing the creation of state insurance exchanges. Furthermore, all individuals not already covered by a private employer plan or public program, such as Medicaid, must purchase their own health insurance policy or pay a penalty to the Internal Revenue Service.[33] This is the so-called individual mandate.

Although before the law was passed Obama insisted that an individual who liked his existing health insurance policy would be able to keep it, this was a deliberate falsehood. In truth, the law required that all insurance policies offer "essential health benefits" as determined and dictated by the Obama administration.[34] Consequently, many existing private policies have been or will be discontinued, severely limiting available health-care options for consumers.

In fact, Obamacare opened the door to infinite future governmental directives and commands covering all aspects of health-care and medical services. For example, the federal government now determines who insurance companies must cover and what benefits they must offer. It prevents insurance companies from denying coverage to people who are already ill or charging higher premiums for those who have greater risk factors. It also puts caps on the out-of-pocket amounts that insurance companies can charge policyholders. These mandates and many more will obviously make it increasingly difficult for insurance companies to remain financially viable. Obamacare's architects attempted to ameliorate the cost of some of these mandates by forcing younger, healthy individuals to buy insurance they may neither want nor need. Younger people, who, as a group, are healthier and less likely to use health-care services, are subsidizing Obamacare, just as they are subsidizing Medicare and Social Security. Even so, Obamacare is not financially viable. Thus, premiums for private coverage continue to rise appreciably. In 2014, health insurance brokers in the individual and small group markets reported that average annual premiums increased by 11 percent (small group) and

12 percent (individual), with much higher increases in some states: Delaware and California, for example, had 100 percent and 53 percent increases, respectively.[35]

Obamacare's advocates also insisted that if passed it would help contain costs. But the experience of Medicare shows otherwise. Massachusetts Institute of Technology (MIT) economist Amy Finkelstein studied the early effects of Medicare on health-care costs and determined that by 1970, within only a few years of its initial passage, it caused a 37 percent increase in hospital spending.[36] A major selling point of Obamacare was that once individuals without insurance were finally covered—for example, through Medicaid expansion—they would no longer go to emergency rooms (ERs) for care. ERs are required by federal law to provide care to everyone, regardless of whether a person has insurance or the ability to pay. ERs are also a very expensive way to receive medical treatment. The Robert Wood Johnson Foundation found that the average ER visit costs $580 more than a trip to the doctor's office.[37] Unfortunately, the early results after Obamacare's passage show a spike in visits to ERs for medical treatment.[38] Among the reasons is that although Medicare and Medicaid claim to provide better "access to health insurance," they cannot guarantee access to a doctor. Not all doctors can afford to keep their practices afloat when Medicare reimburses their services and costs at significantly lower rates. A survey of doctors in 2013 found that only 45.7 percent accepted Medicaid patients.[39] This is not a new development. The same survey showed that in the past ten years, the rate has fluctuated between 50 and 55 percent.[40] And the situation is getting worse.

The Associated Press reported that "A survey [in 2014] by The Physicians Foundation found that 81 percent of doctors describe themselves as either over-extended or at full capacity, and 44 percent said they planned to cut back on the number of patients they see, retire, work part-time, or close their practice to new patients. At the same time, insurance companies have routinely limited the number of doctors and providers on their plans as a way to cut costs. The result has further restricted some patients' ability to get appointments quickly."[41]

Significantly, Obamacare drains $716 billion from Medicare, mostly from the funds used to reimburse hospitals and private health insurers, thereby further weakening a system that is already teetering on the brink of financial collapse and putting an even tighter squeeze on health-care providers.[42]

Amazingly, there is a longer-term plan in the works that would drag the rest of the private health-care system under the control of the federal government. In his first months in office, Obama suggested to the *New York Times* that he did not believe his aging grandmother should have had expensive hip replacement surgery because she did not have much longer to live. He said, "Whether, sort of in the aggregate, society making those decisions to give my grandmother, or everybody else's aging grandparents or parents, a hip replacement when they're terminally ill is a sustainable model, is a very difficult question." This issue was "a huge driver of cost" because "the chronically ill and those toward the end of their lives are accounting for potentially 80 percent of the total health care bill out here." When asked what could be done, Obama suggested further centralizing medical decisions under yet another federal or federally sponsored committee or bureau of supposed experts:

> Well, I think that there is going to have to be a conversation that is guided by doctors, scientists, ethicists. *And then there is going to have to be a very difficult democratic conversation that takes place. It is very difficult to imagine the country making those decisions just through the normal political channels.* And that's part of why you have to have some independent group that can give you guidance. It's not determinative, but I think has to be able to give you some guidance.[43] (Italics added)

Obamacare actually created such a group—the so-called Independent Payment Advisory Board (IPAB). The IPAB is a board that will seek "to reduce the per capita rate of growth in Medicare spending" by developing proposals to cut costs.[44] Beginning in 2015, in any year that Medicare's per capita growth rate exceeds the target rate (a formula tied to the growth of the economy), the IPAB would recommend Medicare spending reductions. The IPAB's proposals become law unless Congress passes a statute containing the same amount of savings. The IPAB will cut payment rates for Medicare providers and suppliers. It will be hard for Congress to ignore the IPAB's "recommendations" or even disband it. The secretary of HHS must automatically implement the board's proposals unless Congress affirmatively acts to change them or stop the process. Obamacare provides that the IPAB can only be disbanded by a three-fifths vote of the members of Congress. Given the filibuster rule in the Senate, which essentially requires three-fifths of senators to pass legislation, and the president's veto authority, which requires two-thirds of the members of Congress to override, there is little doubt that the overwhelming majority of the IPAB's decisions will be irreversible despite the misleading implication that Congress will have the final word.

There is also no doubt that major market-oriented reforms and overhauls are required immediately to address unsustainable federal health-care entitlements and avoid the devastating economic and societal consequences awaiting younger people and future generations from decades of extravagance, political manipulation, and rampant bureaucratic intervention in the private health-care system. But rather than disentangle from the federal Leviathan, the recent imposition of Obamacare demonstrates that ideology trumps rationality and the statists' impulse for even more coercive and disastrous designs are never quenched.

As the late philosopher, economist, and Nobel laureate Friedrich Hayek wrote in *The Road to Serfdom*, "The state should confine itself to establishing rules applying to general types of situations and should allow the individuals freedom in everything which depends on the circumstances of time and place, because only the individuals concerned in each instance can fully know these circumstances and adapt their actions to them. If the individuals are able to use their knowledge effectively in making plans, they must be able to predict actions of the state which may affect these plans. But if the actions of the state are to be predictable, they must be determined by rules fixed independently of the concrete circumstances which can be neither foreseen nor taken into account beforehand; and the particular effects of such actions will be unpredictable. If, on the other hand, the state were to direct the individual's actions so as to achieve particular ends, its actions would have to be decided on the basis of the full circumstances of the moment and would therefore be unpredictable. *Hence the familiar fact that the more the state 'plans,' the more difficult planning becomes for the individual.*"[45] (Italics in original)

The combination of runaway government-induced costs and the accompanying tightening and concentration of federal bureaucratic control over the most intimate decisions about an individual's health, and the exacerbation of these conditions as time goes on, plus the deleterious effects such a Rube Goldberg apparatus with labyrinthine rules and regulations have on the quality and timeliness of medical services, augur very poorly for the health, wealth, and overall well-being of younger people and future generations.

## FIVE

## ON EDUCATION

EDUCATION IS SUPPOSED TO be about the improvement and well-being of the next generation. Learning is supposed to be about seeking and discovering the truth by pursuing evidence and knowledge and applying intelligence, experience, and reason to issues and problem-solving. Unfortunately, the rising generation is the victim of an exceedingly expensive and inferior public education, too often driven by statist ideology and objectives, academic fads and social experimentation, and administrative and bureaucratic empire building.

In fiscal year 2012, the Census Bureau reports that federal, state, and local governments cumulatively spent more than $600 billion, or an average of $10,608 per student per year, on public education. The range of spending spanned from

$19,552 per pupil in New York State to $6,206 per student in Utah.[1] And these figures are off slightly from the high-water marks in 2010, when the country spent $12,743 per student per year, kindergarten through twelfth grade.[2] Also in 2012, of the $600 billion, public elementary and secondary school systems spent nearly $420 billion on salaries, wages, and benefits, over $39 billion on capital outlays, plus over $406 billion on accumulated debt.[3]

Respecting public school teacher compensation, Andrew G. Biggs, a resident scholar at the American Enterprise Institute (AEI), and Jason Richwine, a senior policy analyst in the Center for Data Analysis at the Heritage Foundation, undertook a comparative analysis study of teacher and non-teacher compensation in 2011 and concluded that "public-school teacher salaries are comparable to those paid to similarly skilled private sector workers, but that more generous fringe benefits for public-school teachers, including greater job security, make total compensation 52 percent greater than fair market levels, equivalent to more than $120 billion in overcharges to taxpayers each year." Apart from overall school system debt, in 2014 the National Council on Teacher Quality reported that state teacher pension systems had a total of $499 billion in unfunded liabilities, an increase of $100 billion in just two years.[4]

Spending levels on kindergarten to twelfth-grade public education are even more striking when compared with those of other developed "first world" nations on the international stage. According to the Organization for Economic Cooperation and Development (OECD), only Luxembourg and Norway spend more per child than the United States, and Luxembourg's spending is skewed because of its status as an international financial center with a very small national population. All other countries the OECD surveyed spend dramatically less than the United States.[5]

Despite the enormous and unparalleled costs, America's public schools are performing poorly and many are failing. The Program for International Student Assessment (PISA) is an international organization affiliated with the OECD that periodically administers standardized proficiency tests to fourth graders and fifteen-year-olds in schools in sixty-five countries. These results are analyzed and made available to participating countries for near- and long-term education budgeting and planning. The PISA 2012 results were published recently, and they point to a failing American educational system. In math literacy, only 9 percent of American fifteen-year olds finished in the top ranks of proficiency (level 5 or above, out of six levels). This is a lower percentage of top performers than their opposite numbers in 27 countries. It is also a higher share than students in 22 nations, roughly equivalent to those in 13 more nations, and lower than the average score developed by the OECD of 13 percent of students in the top-performing category.[6] Twenty-six percent of students scored at the level 2 or lower, which PISA established as the lowest passing level of proficiency for the testing continuum. The average score was 23 percent. Students in 26 nations scored higher and in 29 nations finished with lower scores. Nine nations basically tied with the proficiency level in the United States. The average test score of American students was 481, also below the OECD average score of 494. Again, this was lower than 29 nations and higher than 26 others.[7]

Only 7 percent of American fifteen-year-olds scored in the top levels of science proficiency, which was close to the average of 8 percent—lower than 167 education systems and higher than only 27.[8] Eighteen percent of American students finished at level 2 or below—better than only 21 education systems and worse than 29 systems. The results were similar for reading proficiency.[9]

The standardized Scholastic Aptitude Tests (SAT) for 2013 paint an equally grim picture. Only 43 percent of the 1.66 million students who took the test scored high enough to be classified as "college ready." What is worse, this is the fifth year in a row that fewer than half of the young people who took the test scored above 1550, the threshold for demonstrating the capability to maintain a grade point average (GPA) of B-minus or better in a four-year degree college or university.[10]

According to the United States Department of Education (DOE), the 2013 National Assessment of Educational Progress (NAEP)[11] reports that only 26 percent of the nation's twelfth graders are proficient in math and only 38 percent are proficient in reading. There is also a twenty-nine percentage point gap between the reading proficiency of white and black twelfth-grade students. And these numbers are unchanged since 2009.[12]

Even the Armed Services Vocational Battery, which is a group of tests given to determine whether servicemen who want to join a Special Forces unit are minimally qualified, reveals serious educational problems. Sixty-six percent of all applicants fail to meet the minimum educational standards on the tests. Eighty-six percent of African-American applicants and 79 percent of Hispanic applicants fail.[13]

In plain English, the immense investment of tax dollars in a vast government-run educational infrastructure is buying young people a poor education. The data demonstrate there is no overall correlation between the dramatic spending increases in public education during the last several decades and academic achievement. Indeed, in 2014, Andrew Coulson, director of the Cato Institute's Center for Educational Freedom, examined this precise point. He undertook a careful study that, as he explains, "adjusts state SAT [Scholastic Aptitude Test] score averages for factors such as participation rate and student demographics, which are known to affect outcomes, then validates the results against recent state-level National Assessment of Educational Progress (NAEP) test scores. This produces continuous, state-representative estimated SAT score trends reaching back to 1972. The present paper charts these trends against both inflation-adjusted per-pupil spending and the raw, unadjusted SAT results, providing an unprecedented perspective on American education inputs and outcomes over the past 40 years."[14]

Coulson concluded that "In general, the findings are not encouraging. Adjusted state SAT scores have declined by an average of 3 percent. This echoes the picture of stagnating achievement among American 17-year-olds painted by the Long Term Trends portion of the National Assessment of Educational Progress, a series of tests administered to a nationally representative sample of students since 1970. That disappointing record comes despite a more than doubling in inflation-adjusted per pupil public-school spending over the same period (the average state spending increase was 120 percent). Consistent with those patterns, there has been essentially no correlation between what states have spent on education and their measured academic outcomes. In other words, America's educational productivity appears to have collapsed, at least as measured by the NAEP and the SAT."[15]

As well, the nature of the teaching profession has fundamentally transformed. Since the 1960s the nation's two largest teachers' unions, the National Education Association (NEA) and the American Federation of Teachers (AFT), have become enormously powerful political forces, aligning almost exclusively with the Democratic Party.[16] In exchange for supporting laws and policies that empower these unions, the union leaders have succeeded in securing from elected politicians privileges and benefits for teachers that too often are not in the best interests of the students or the community. For example, while there are undoubtedly many excellent teachers in school districts throughout the nation, the NEA and AFT have aggressively opposed serious and enforceable standards of merit and competency for their members, making accountability in the classroom nearly impossible, while steadfastly defending tenure and poorly performing teachers.[17] The late, longtime president of the AFT, Albert Shanker, once admitted that "In our system, we have a large number of teachers who have not reached even very low levels of literacy and numeracy."[18]

A recent case in California directly tied teacher tenure and firing policies to a bad education. In June 2014, in a rare ruling, a state judge held in *Vergara* v. *California* that teacher tenure, firing, and layoff laws, which make it extremely difficult to remove bad teachers, violated the state constitution.[19] Poor and minority students were denied equal protection because they were more likely to have "grossly ineffective" teachers.

Evidence has been elicited in this trial of the specific effect of the grossly ineffective teachers on students. The evidence is compelling. Indeed, it shocks the conscience. Based on a massive study, Dr. Chetty testified that a single year in a classroom with a grossly ineffective teacher costs students $1.4 million in lifetime earnings per classroom. Based on a 4 year study, Dr. Kane testified that students in LAUSD [Los Angeles Unified School District] who are taught by a teacher in the bottom 5% of competence lose

9.54 months of learning in a single year compared to students with average teachers.[20]

The judge found the firing process "so complex, time consuming and expensive as to make an effective, efficient yet fair dismissal of a grossly ineffective teacher illusory."[21]

In addition to the problem of teacher competency there is the malignancy of statist-driven political conformity, ideological indoctrination, social engineering, and academic experimentation that have suffused public schools with such agendas as multiculturalism, global warming, and the distortion of American history, among other things.[22] Furthermore, academic fads have been forced upon successive generations of elementary and secondary school students, including the "New Math," the "Open Classroom," "Values Clarification," "Cooperative Learning," "Outcome-Based Education," "No Child Left Behind," and more recently "Common Core" and "Race to the Top," for which trillions of dollars have been and are being wasted on inferior educational outcomes. Even the once-heralded school lunch program is not safe from statist overreach, where billions of dollars are spent on federally mandated lunches that many students refuse to eat.[23]

For those students who move on to a postsecondary education, the circumstances worsen. For starters, the price of a college education is often financially debilitating. Seventy-one percent who graduated in the last few years owe an average of

$29,400 in outstanding student loans. As of 2012, the cost of a college degree had grown 40 percent since 2001.[24]

The numbers are even worse when compared to a longer historical perspective. In 1963–64, the average tuition, room and board, and fees for a four-year institution—public, private, or for-profit—was $1,248. In 2013, the figure was $20,234.

The cost to attend college is rising so fast that, according to the Federal Reserve Bank of New York, the amount of outstanding student loans in the United States, as reported on credit reports, grew to $1.13 trillion in the third quarter of 2014, an increase of approximately $100 billion from the prior year. And around 11 percent of the student loan debt was more than ninety days delinquent or in default.[25] Overall, about one-third of borrowers with student loans owned by the DOE are more than five days late on their payments.[26]

There is also something unique about college tuition debt that does not occur with other kinds of debt (credit card debt, auto loan debt, and so on). First, it is the fastest-growing type of indebtedness in the country. The Pew Research Center found that, in households headed by young adults, those without tuition debt had more than seven times the overall net worth of similar households with student loans ($64,700 to $8,700).[27] Those with student loan debt also had nearly double the overall indebtedness of those who had no such loans ($137,010 to $73,250).[28] The Federal Reserve's Survey of Consumer Finances, as reported by the *Wall Street Journal*, found that "student debt now burdens 41.4 percent of those under 35. In 2007, only 33.6 percent of people under 35 had loans and in 1998 it rose to 23.3 percent. The balances of those who borrow have been growing as well, to $17,300 in this survey, up from $13,000 in 2007 and $10,000 in 1998. For those beginning careers, thousands of dollars in debt can take years for net worth to climb into positive territory."[29]

Tuition, fees, and room and board costs for colleges and universities of all stripes rose faster than the rate of inflation each year for more than the last thirty years. These increases came whether in good economic times or bad, or whether the demand for college degrees was waxing or waning. Nevertheless, colleges and universities have established some of the most prodigious fund-raising operations in existence. The top twenty richest American universities all have endowment funds of about $5 billion or more. The richest, Harvard University, has an endowment fund in excess of $32 billion (down from more than $36 billion before the Great Recession).[30] But most of these institutions are not eager to use their own funds to defray costs.

America postsecondary education has become a huge industry. Colleges and universities employed about 850,000 people, or about 1.5 percent of the total workforce, in 1960, including administrators, faculty, and support personnel. According to the Bureau of Labor Statistics (BLS), there were about 4 million people working on the nation's campuses as of 2009, or approximately 3 percent of the nation's workers.[31] Of those nearly 4 million people, 1.7 million were faculty, professors, and instructors. The rest were administrators and support personnel.[32]

Employees at these institutions are also well compensated. As of March 2010, the average per-hour cost for employee compensation for college and university workers was $44.82. Just over $31.12 of that sum covered wages and salaries, and the remaining $13.70 per hour went toward benefits.[33] According to the BLS, the average employer cost for employee compensation in March 2014 was $31.93 per hour, wages and salaries accounting for $21.96, with the remaining $9.97 going toward employee benefits.[34]

Another significant factor for the soaring cost of college tuition is the irresponsible and extravagant spending on major construction projects. In 2012, the *New York Times* reported that "A decade-long spending binge to build academic buildings, dormitories and recreational facilities—some of them inordinately lavish to attract students—has left colleges and universities saddled with large amounts of debt. Oftentimes, students are stuck picking up the bill. Overall debt levels more than doubled from 2000 to 2011 at the more than 500 institutions rated by Moody's, according to inflation-adjusted data. . . . In the same time, the amount of cash, pledged gifts and investments that colleges maintain declined more than 40 percent relative to the amount they owe."[35] The *Times* added: "The debate about indebtedness has focused on students and graduates who have borrowed tens of thousands of dollars and are struggling to keep up with their payments. Nearly one in every six borrowers with a student loan balance is in default. But some colleges and universities have also borrowed heavily, spending money on vast expansions and amenities aimed at luring better students; student unions with movie theaters and wine bars; workout facilities with climbing walls and 'lazy rivers'; and dormitories with single rooms and private baths. Spending on instruction has grown at a much slower pace, studies have shown. Students end up covering some, if not most, of the debt payments in the form of higher tuition, room and board, and special assessments, while in other instances state taxpayers pick up the costs. Debt has ballooned at colleges across the board—public and private, elite and obscure. While Harvard is the wealthiest university in the country, it also has $6 billion in debt, the most of any private college, the data compiled by Moody's shows."[36] As of 2011, colleges and universities have racked up a debt bill of $205 billion.[37]

Indeed, "[o]utstanding debt at the 224 public universities rated by Moody's grew to $122 billion in 2011, from $53 billion in inflation-adjusted dollars in 2000. At the 281 private universities rated by Moody's, debt increased to $83 billion, from $40 billion, in that period. Rather than deplete their endowments, some colleges borrowed to help pay bills after the financial crisis, but most borrowing was for capital projects. Since 2000, the amount paid in interest and principal has increased 67 percent at public institutions, to $9.3 billion in 2011, and it increased 62 percent at private institutions, to $5 billion last year."[38]

The statist answer to this unmitigated financial disaster is, in part, the effective nationalization of student loan debt. Language added to the massive Patient Protection and Affordable Care Act of 2010, or Obamacare, made the federal Department of Education the students' loan officer. It will now make nearly 100 percent of future student loans, which will be federally guaranteed by the taxpayer. Of course, this does nothing to reduce the cost of postsecondary education. Nor is the federal government in a position to assume even more debt. Moreover, *Politico* reports that "buried deep in its 2016 budget proposal, the Obama administration revealed . . . that its student loan program had a $21.8 billion shortfall last year, apparently the largest ever recorded for any government credit program. The main cause of the shortfall was President Barack Obama's recent efforts to provide relief for borrowers drowning in student debt, reforms that have already begun to reduce loan payments to the government."[39] In fact, "direct government loans alone increased 44 percent over the last two years. . . ."[40] Furthermore, "[s]everal reports by Barclays Capital have warned that Obama's generosity to borrowers could leave the student loan program as much as $250 billion in the hole over the next decade."[41] Thus, rather than addressing the root causes of reckless "education" spending and borrowing, these efforts have ensured that the system will bloat further and eventually rupture.

Then there is the matter of actual education. Despite

claims of "academic freedom," like the public school system postsecondary education is rife with the ideological viewpoints of utopian statists. In 2011, over 62 percent of faculty members who teach full-time at undergraduate colleges and universities in America identified themselves as either "liberal" (50.3 percent) or "far left" (12.4 percent) on the political spectrum, up from about 56 percent in 2008.[42] In 2008, 47 percent of faculty members surveyed identified as "liberal" while 8.8 percent labeled themselves as "far left." Conversely, only 11.5 percent of faculty surveyed self-identified as "conservative" and just .4 percent as "far right." This was down from 2008, when 15.2 percent accepted the title of "conservative" and only .7% percent "far right."[43]

The statist ideological orthodoxy is reflected not merely in the content of professorial lectures, but also in the coursework and textbooks selected by the professors. This is particularly prominent in, although certainly not exclusive to, classrooms where the humanities and social sciences are taught. Here is but one example, from a textbook, *You May Ask Yourself: Thinking Like a Sociologist*, used at the College of William and Mary, and at universities and colleges throughout the country:

> By now you should be wary of any social institution that is hailed supreme because it is "more natural." You should be skeptical of any family arrangement that is deemed more functional than another, and you should hold the traditional family at a critical distance, especially consid-

ering the experiences of women, African Americans, gays and lesbians, the poor, the mainstream, and the marginalized. Under the "post modern family condition," as Judith Stacey calls it, clear rules no longer exist in our complex, diversified, and sometimes messy post industrial society (1996). Gone are the ruling days of the normative Nelsons. Families today take on many shapes and sizes that best fit their members' needs and they are defined not by blood ties but by the quality of relationships. Let us count the ways.[44]

Daniel B. Klein and Charlotta Stern, in an article in the *Independent Review, A Journal of Political Economy*, place much of the blame for this "groupthink" at the feet of specific departments and department heads, which perpetuate an ideological closed-mindedness. They argue that the faculty in a given department is less governed by the zeitgeist of the larger institutional community than by the modus vivendi of the specific department and, more broadly, the profession in which it operates. The values of the individuals at the apex of that department usually dictate the standards and norms under which the faculty functions. Most often, this means that ideas or opinions that contradict those held by the leaders of the department are less likely to be published or even expressed openly by faculty, and tenure may also be offered or denied based on loyalty to the predicates of the department. There is also an incestuous network of graduates from the top departments in different fields who hire fellow alumni as they move into the highest positions in departments at other colleges and universities. Klein and Stern cite a survey of the most prestigious two hundred economics departments around the world. "Graduates from the top five departments account for roughly one-third of all faculty hired in other departments surveyed. The top 20 departments account for roughly 70% of the total."[45]

Even worse, "of the 430 full-time faculty employed by the top 20 sociology departments . . . only 7 (less than 2 percent) received their PhDs from a non-top 20 department." "In the field of law," Richard Redding finds, "a third of all new teachers (hired in law schools between 1996 and 2000) graduated from either Harvard (18 percent) or Yale (15 percent); another third graduated from other top-12 schools, and 20 percent graduated from other top-25 law schools."[46]

The enforcement of ideological groupthink extends beyond the faculty. College and university campuses are now among the least tolerant institutions for inquiry and debate. Too frequently they accept or even encourage an atmosphere of discomfort, intimidation, or militancy in promotion of the statist orthodoxy. The purpose is primarily political indoctrination of the sort that is hostile to the civil society and America's heritage. And toward this end, the campus and classroom atmosphere narrows the scope of what is considered legitimate thought or opinion, dismisses or derides more traditional viewpoints that challenge statist convention, and disregard outright the perspective of individuals who are not identifiable members of a politically preferred group—either by birth or by belief.

Even as students graduate from colleges and universities, most are treated to one last speech from a statist spouting ideological boilerplate. According to Young America's Foundation, as reported by Fox News, in 2015 "liberal speakers outnumbered conservatives by at least 6 to 1 at the nation's top 100 schools as ranked by *U.S. News & World Report.* Among the top 10 of the list, none hosted conservative speakers."[47]

At the end of his book, *The Closing of the American Mind,* the late philosopher, educator, and author Allan Bloom questioned whether the nation's failing educational system, most notably higher education, could "constitute or reconstitute the idea of an educated human being. . . ."[48]

> This is the American moment in world history, the one for which we shall forever be judged. Just as in politics the responsibility for the fate of freedom in the world has devolved upon our regime, so the fate of philosophy in the world has devolved upon our universities, and the two are related as they have never been before. The gravity of our given task is great, and it is very much in doubt how the future will judge our stewardship.[49]

There are salient realities that very few in the academy will acknowledge. The most prominent is that education is not

supposed to be about administrators and educational bureaucrats, labor unions, tenured educators, improvident construction projects, and statist indoctrination. It is supposed to be
about the enrichment and improvement of young people and
society. Students are not lab rats to be subjected to endless
educational experiments; they are not Pavlov's dog to be con-
ditioned as societal malcontents; and they and their families
(and the taxpayers) are not cash cows for reckless spending
and debt assumption. The failure of American education is an
unforgivable dereliction of one generation to the next.

SIX

---

# ON IMMIGRATION

WHEN THE ISSUE OF immigration is raised or debated, the one group rarely considered or consulted is the group most adversely affected by current immigration policies—the rising generation. Therefore, it is pivotal to examine the nation's immigration affairs in the context of the well-being of younger people and future generations.

For more than two centuries, the United States has attracted immigrants from all over the world. America's civil society, in which societal and cultural traditions and values have served as a beacon to humanity, has historically inspired millions to come to America in search of a better life. In the seventeenth and eighteenth centuries, immigrants from Europe came to the United States seeking, among other things, religious freedom. In the nineteenth century, immigrants from countries such as Ireland, Italy, and Germany were mostly escaping famine and oppression. In the twentieth century, America welcomed those fleeing communism and despotism. However, as the late Harvard professor Dr. Samuel Huntington explained in his book *Who Are We? The Challenges to America's National Identity*, "America has been a nation of restricted and interrupted immigration as much as it has been a nation of immigration."[1] It may surprise some to learn that in the past, each successive wave of immigration was followed by a period of time where the flow of aliens ebbed as more recent arrivals assimilated into the American way of life.

For example, from 1901 through 1910, approximately 8.8 million people immigrated to the United States. The United States Census Bureau reports that between 1911 and 1920, there were 5.7 million immigrants, and between 1921 and 1930, there were a little over 4 million immigrants.[2] The 1930s through 1970s experienced periods of immigration followed by integration and assimilation. About five hundred thousand individuals immigrated into the United States between 1931 and 1940; between 1941 and 1950, a little over one million; between 1951 and 1960, approximately 2.5 million came to America; and between 1961 and 1970, there were some 3.3 million immigrants.[3]

However, today there is no period of assimilation between immigration flows. Rather, the flow of immigrants coming to America for more than forty years has been unprecedented and uninterrupted, with no end in sight. In the last decade and a half alone, from 2000 through 2014, 14 million new permanent legal immigrants were admitted to the United States in addition to the surge of millions of illegal immigrants.[4] The Migration Policy Institute reports that 2013 estimates from the Census Bureau put the U.S. immigrant population at more than 41.3 million, or 13 percent, of the total U.S. population of 316.1 million. Between 2012 and 2013, the foreign-born population increased by about 523,000, or 1.3 percent. U.S. immigrants and their U.S.-born children now number approximately 80 million persons, or one-quarter of the overall U.S. population.[5]

In *Liberty and Tyranny*, I explained how this wave of immigration was triggered by the 1965 Hart-Celler Act, which introduced a system of chain migration—that is, awarding preferences to family members of citizens and resident aliens. This was a radical departure from past immigration policy. For the first time, the law empowered immigrants in the United States to elicit further immigration into the country through family reunification. The late author Theodore White wrote that "the Immigration Act of 1965 changed all previous patterns, and in so doing, probably changed the future of America. . . . [I]t was noble, revolutionary—and probably the most thoughtless of the many acts of the Great Society."[6] As a result, in subsequent years immigrants have been poorer, less educated, and less skilled than those who preceded them—a pattern that continues today.[7]

Moreover, President Barack Obama, as a matter of unilateral executive policy, and in contravention of existing immigration law, has severely weakened deportation efforts. A
report issued by Senator Jeff Sessions (R, Ala.) reveals that "interior deportations have fallen 23 percent since [2014] alone,
and have been halved since 2011—when then–Immigration
and Customs Enforcement Director (ICE) [John] Morton issued the so-called Morton Memos exempting almost all illegal immigrants from enforcement and removal operations.
The effective result of the Administration's non-enforcement
policy is that anyone in the world who manages to get into
the interior of the United States—by any means, including
overstaying a visa—is free to live, work, and claim benefits in
the United States at Americans' expense."[8] In fact, Obama
has gone further. In an unprecedented and unconstitutional
act, he issued the so-called Deferred Action for Parents of
Americans and Lawful Permanent Residents (DAPA), which
seeks to legalize nearly 5 million illegal aliens. As the *Washington Post* editorialized: "Mr. Obama's move flies in the face
of congressional intent."[9] For now, the federal courts, at the
request of numerous states, have stayed the implementation
of Obama's fiat. The matter is likely to be resolved by the U.S.
Supreme Court.

As Dr. Huntington described, the massive influx of aliens
has been rationalized, in part, by what European scholars have
promoted and conceptualized as "societal security." It is an

attempt to justify the deleterious effect unfettered, unassimilated immigration has on a society. It refers to "the ability of
a society to persist in its essential character under changing
conditions and possible or actual threats"; "the sustainabil-
ity, within acceptable conditions for evolution, of traditional
patterns of language, culture, association, and religious and
national identity and custom." Dr. Huntington wrote that it
"is concerned above all with identity, the ability of a people to
maintain their culture, institutions, and way of life."[10] However, in the United States, he added, "America has . . . been a
nation of immigration *and* assimilation, and assimilation has
meant Americanization. Now, however, immigrants are different; the institutions and processes related to assimilation are
different; and, most importantly, America is different. . . ."[11]
"Assimilation of current immigrants is . . . likely to be slower,
less complete, and different from the assimilation of earlier
immigrants. Assimilation no longer necessarily means Americanization."[12]

If assimilation no longer means Americanization, then in
what kind of society will younger people and future generations live? Princeton University professor Dr. Douglas Massey
points out that as a result of continuing high levels of immigration "the character of ethnicity will be determined relatively
more by immigrants and relatively less by later generations,
shifting the balance of ethnic identity toward the language,
culture, and ways of life in the sending society."[13] Therefore,

immigration without assimilation and Americanization un-
dercuts the civil society as ethnic, racial, and religious groups
self-segregate. The problem is magnified further when a nation
abandons its own culture to promote multiculturalism, dual
citizenship, bilingualism, and so on, and institutes countless
policies and laws promoting and protecting the practices of
balkanized groups and their infinite array of grievances.

The Center for Immigration Studies (CIS) explains that
as of 2010, there were approximately 40 million legal and illegal immigrants residing in the United States—an increase
of 28 percent from 2000.[14] One in five public school students
(or 10.4 million) are from an immigrant home. It is further
estimated that 28 percent of all immigrants are in the country illegally.[15] The Congressional Budget Office (CBO) has
performed an analysis of the latest effort to grant amnesty to
illegal immigrants and concluded that it would increase the
immigrant population by about 10 million (approximately
3 percent) in 2023 and some 16 million people (about 4 percent) by 2033.[16]

Open-ended immigration takes a considerable toll on the
job prospects of younger and less-skilled workers, as well as
college-educated graduates. Typically, younger workers (those
between the ages of sixteen and twenty-nine) are competing
with recent immigrants for similar jobs. Many younger people
begin working as waiters, construction workers, or grocery-
store clerks. These are the types of jobs many illegal immigrants also seek. "How can that be?" you might ask. After all,

as the argument goes, illegal immigrants do jobs Americans will not do. For example, the United States Chamber of Commerce advocates widespread amnesty to enable its members— mostly large corporations—to "utilize immigrant labor when U.S. workers are said not to be available."[17] The National Restaurant Association supports amnesty, in part, because "[t]here are too many jobs Americans won't do."[18] The Independent Institute, a libertarian group, has insisted that low-skilled immigrants "do jobs that wouldn't exist if the immigrants weren't there to do them."[19] It claims that immigrants "aren't substitutes for American labor."[20] They "free up American labor to do jobs where it is more productive."[21] The facts demonstrate otherwise.

Using the federal government's own statistics, CIS explains that the Census Bureau has identified what it classifies as 472 civilian occupations. Of those occupations, six are considered majority immigrant (legal and illegal). Those six occupations amount to about 1 percent of the total workforce. However, jobs that are stereotypically thought to comprise mainly immigrants actually comprise mostly American citizens. Maids and housekeepers are 51 percent citizen; taxi drivers are 58 percent citizen; butchers are 63 percent citizen; landscapers or grounds workers are 64 percent citizen; construction workers are 66 percent citizen; porters, bellhops, and concierges are 72 percent citizen; and janitors are 73 percent citizen.[22]

Moreover, 16.5 million citizens have jobs in the sixty-seven occupations composed of a significant percentage of im-

migrants (25 percent or more).[23] In other words, millions of
Americans work in jobs that are incorrectly but widely considered "immigrant-type." These "high-immigrant occupations"
are mainly "lower-wage jobs" requiring "little formal education." Notably, citizens in "high-immigrant occupations" have
a much higher unemployment rate than citizens who work in
jobs with a smaller percentage of immigrants.[24] The logical
conclusion is that although Americans hold more of the jobs
in occupations that have a higher percentage of immigrants,
untold numbers of Americans, particularly younger and less
skilled, are having more difficulty finding jobs in these occupations as immigrants are filling a growing percentage of them.

As it happens, on April 22, 2015, the Congressional
Research Service (CRS) reported to the Senate Judiciary
Committee, in part, that "Between 1970 and 2013, the
estimated foreign-born population in the United States increased from 9,740,000 to 41,348,066, respectively, an increase
of 31,608,066 persons, representing a percentage increase of
324.5% over this 43 year period; . . . [t]he reported income of
the bottom 90% of tax filers in the United States decreased
from an average of $33,621 in 1970 to $30,980 in 2013 for
an aggregate decline of $2,641 or a percent decline of 7.9%
over this 43 year period; . . . [t]he share of income held by the
bottom 90% of the U.S. income distribution declined from
68.5% in 1970 to 53.0% in 2013, an absolute decline of 15.5
percentage points over this 43 year period."[25]

Thus, statist immigration policies centered on endless waves of legal and illegal immigration have contributed significantly to the income deterioration of low-income American earners and the "inequality gap" between rich and poor, which the statists claim to abhor.

Although it is also repeatedly alleged that America must open immigration further to accommodate increased numbers of high-skilled and high-tech workers because the country is supposedly failing to produce enough homegrown college graduates with science, technology, engineering, or math (STEM) skills to fill the demands of the fast-paced market, this, too, is false. Despite America's mediocre education system, the evidence demonstrates that enough college students in the STEM disciplines are graduating to fill the market's demand. A thorough analysis by scholars Hal Salzman, Daniel Kuehn, and B. Lindsay Lowell from the Economic Policy Institute found that "for every two students that U.S. colleges graduate with STEM degrees, only one is hired into a STEM job."[26]

The report further states that "of the computer science graduates not entering the [information technology] workforce, 32 percent say it is because IT jobs are unavailable, and 53 percent say they found better job opportunities outside of IT occupations."[27] The three scholars conclude this indicates "that the supply of graduates (in STEM related fields) is substantially larger than the demand for them in industry."[28] Indeed, while demanding that the federal government substantially increase the number of high-skilled and high-tech immigrants in the country, Hewlett-Packard, Cisco, American Express, Procter and Gamble, T-Mobile, and Microsoft recently slashed tens of thousands of employees.[29] The Census Bureau reports that "74 percent of those who have a bachelor's degree in science, technology, engineering and math—commonly referred to as STEM—are not employed in STEM occupations."[30]

Furthermore, in the STEM-related industries "wages have remained flat" and are "hovering around their late 1990's levels."[31] That means the salaries of professionals in these fields have not increased in the last sixteen years. While salaries have not increased, "the flow of guestworkers has increased over the past decade and continues to rise."[32] "The annual inflows of guestworkers amount to one-third to one-half the number of all new IT job holders."[33]

Salzman, Kuehn, and Lowell conclude that "Immigration policies that facilitate large flows of guestworkers will supply labor at wages that are too low to induce significant increases in supply from the domestic workforce."[34] Consequently, immigration policies designed to increase the number of high-tech workers ensure that wages are kept lower than they otherwise might be.

At the other end of the formal education spectrum, the Bureau of Labor Statistics (BLS) reports that high school dropouts "face a much higher unemployment rate than the national average." In 2012–13, dropouts had an unemployment rate of 27.9 percent.[35] The Foundation for American Immigration Reform (FAIR) found that dropouts have been identified as the group "who face competition for jobs most directly from illegal aliens."[36] The number of unemployed citizens "without a high school diploma increased by 18.7 percent while the number of unemployed foreign-born persons decreased by 24.8 percent."[37] Despite the supposed economic recovery "following the Great Recession, employers continued to favor illegal alien labor despite millions of less-educated Americans who were unemployed."[38]

Clearly, current immigration policies and trends are devastating to America's younger people and future generations.

Andrew Sum and Ishwar Khatiwada, scholars with the Center for Labor Market Statistics at Northeastern University, explain that employment as a teen and young adult is particularly important and has a "wide array of private and social economic and educational benefits."[39] High unemployment among these younger people (like high unemployment generally) "reduces the volume of labor inputs into the production process and the level of real output of the U.S. economy."[40] Without a job, younger people lose the opportunity to gain experience and become more valuable for higher-skilled jobs, which they may seek in the future. In fact, the earnings of teens and younger adults are "used to generate additional consumption expenditures on goods and services, thereby raising aggregate demand throughout the economy and the level of employment of other adult workers."[41]

In addition, employment at a young age discourages dropping out of high school. "[A] number of studies of the in high school work experiences of teens have found that youth with some in-school employment experience, especially Black, Hispanic, and economically disadvantaged youths, are less likely to drop out of high school than their peers who do not work during their high school years."[42]

Working at a younger age also benefits those who do not continue their education by attending college. Those who work in high school, "especially those who do not go on to enroll in four year colleges and universities, obtain a smoother transition into the labor market in the first few years after graduation from high school, avoiding problems of long-term idleness."[43] "[T]hose who learn new skills on their jobs, obtain significantly higher hourly earnings on their jobs in the first few years following graduation." In the long term, these individuals "will secure significantly higher annual earning eight to ten years after graduation than their peers who did not work during high school."[44]

Sum and Khatiwada found that youth employment is linked to lower rates of teen pregnancy and reductions in crime, particularly among young men. Simply put, "high rates of idleness among men reduce their work experience and their future earnings potential, thus making criminal activity more attractive."[45]

Joblessness and underemployment among younger people have also changed the family dynamic, making it more difficult for young adults to leave home. For example, Pew Research reports that from 1968 to 2007 the percentage "of young adults living in their parents' home was relatively constant [at about 32 percent]."[46] By 2012, 36 percent of those between the ages of eighteen and thirty-one lived in their parents' home.[47] This "is the highest share in at least four decades and represents a slow but steady increase."[48] Hence, 21.6 million young adults are now living with their parents (up from 18.5 million in 2007).[49]

More broadly, the overall employment trend for citizens is troublesome. CIS shows that 5.7 million more immigrants between the ages of 16 and 65 were working in the first quarter of 2014 than in 2000. Conversely, 127,000 fewer native-born citizens were working in the first quarter of 2014 than in 2000. This is particularly jarring in that during the same period, the total number of native-born citizens between the ages of 16 and 65 increased by more than 16.8 million. Furthermore, from 2000 to 2014, the population of working-age (16–65) individuals grew by 25.7 million (14 percent). Employment, however, only grew by 4 percent. Incredibly, while native-born citizens accounted for 66 percent of the total population growth from 2000 to 2014, immigrants have accounted for 100 percent of employment growth.[50] Therefore, the working-age population in America is growing faster than jobs are being created, and the increasing supply of immigrants makes finding employment far more difficult.

These statistics reflect the larger trend of fewer total

native-born workers in the United States. In 2000, there were approximately 41 million native-born, working-age Americans (those between ages 16 and 65) who were not working. By 2007, that number had risen to 48.2 million. In 2014, the number rose to 58 million.[51] Seventeen million fewer native-born Americans are working today than were working fourteen years ago. The labor force participation rate of 62.9 percent (July of 2014) is lower than any time since 1979.[52] This means that only 62.9 percent, or less than two-thirds of the population, is working.

By all measures, it is more difficult for all citizens, but especially younger people, to find work today than at any time in the last twenty years. Overall job prospects for younger people (in this case, individuals born between 1980 and 2000) are dreadful. In October 2013, FAIR disclosed that half of all unemployed workers were younger people (those between the ages of 16 and 34).[53] The BLS reports that the labor participation rate for younger people between the ages of 16 and 19 in 2012 was 34.3 percent. In 2002, labor participation for civilians in this age cohort was 47.4 percent.[54] The BLS predicts that by 2022, only 27.3 percent of civilians between the ages of 16 and 19 will be working.[55] The labor participation rate for individuals between the ages of 20 and 24 was 70.9 percent in 2012. In 2002, the labor participation rate for civilians in this age group was 76.4 percent; by 2022, the labor participation rate for civilians between these ages will drop to

67.3 percent.[56] Pew Research reveals that in 2012, 63 percent of those between the ages of 18 and 31 had jobs, but this is down from 70 percent of "same-aged counterparts who had jobs in 2007."[57]

In addition to depressing job prospects and wages for American citizens, particularly the rising generation, unconstrained immigration is a major drain on the immense and already broke welfare state. Dr. Milton Friedman, who was sympathetic to open-ended immigration, was also intellectually honest about its impracticability given the federal government's massive welfare and entitlement programs. As he explained: "[I]t is one thing to have free immigration to jobs. It is another thing to have free immigration to welfare. And you cannot have both. If you have a welfare state, if you have a state in which every resident is promised a certain minimal level of income, or a minimum level of subsistence, regardless of whether he works or not, produces it or not. Then it really is an impossible thing."[58] Moreover, as Dr. Huntington observed, there is a pronounced "erosion of the differences between citizens and aliens . . . [which] suggest the central importance of material government benefits for immigrant decisions. Immigrants become citizens not because they are attracted to America's culture and creed, but because they are attracted by government social welfare and affirmative action programs. If these are available to noncitizens, the incentive for citizenship fades."[59] Of course, there are exceptions, including those escaping persecution and tyranny, but increasingly immigrants are drawn to America's social welfare benefits, which the federal government encourages.

The Heritage Foundation's findings underscore the problem. It reports that "On average, unlawful immigrant households received $24,721 per household in government benefits and services in FY 2010. This figure includes direct benefits, means-tested benefits, education, and population-based services received by the household but excludes the cost of public goods, interest on the government debt, and other payments for prior government functions. By contrast, unlawful immigrant households on average paid only $10,334 in taxes. Thus, unlawful immigrant households received $2.40 in benefits and services for each dollar paid in taxes."[60] "All unlawful immigrant households together [in 2010] received $93.7 billion per year in government benefits and services and paid $39.2 billion, yielding an aggregate annual deficit of $54.5 billion."[61]

Under Obama's recent unconstitutional executive amnesty, the CBO concluded that should it be implemented, between 2 million and 2.5 million illegal immigrants will "have received approval for deferred action" by 2017. Therefore, many will become eligible for Social Security, Medicare, and the earned income tax credit. "Those who are approved for deferred action are considered lawfully present in the country but do not gain legal status. However, they can, and most do, receive authorization to work. Because they are deemed lawfully present during the period of their deferred status, they are eligible to receive Medicare and Social Security benefits if they meet the programs' requirements."[62] Those granted deferred status and work permits are also eligible for the earned income tax credit.[63] Therefore, the drain on already hemorrhaging federal entitlements and programs is further exacerbated.

The worst of the statists and their surrogates seek political opportunism and racial balkanization as a means to holding or acquiring governing power.[64] And they are intent on accomplishing these ends through mostly unlawful and unconstitutional means, such as Obama's executive and administrative fiats. Even now, with the expectation that a substantial percentage of newly naturalized aliens would vote for the Democratic Party's 2016 nominee for president, the Department of Homeland Security's Task Force on New Americans is reportedly focusing resources on urging 9 million green card holders (aliens and noncitizens) to become naturalized American citizens as quickly as possible, in hopes of influencing the outcome of the 2016 presidential election.[65] Others perpetuate the myths and outright deceptions about the economic and societal benefits of unrelenting, unassimilated waves of immigration. These are among the forces that are driving the immigration agenda. And they are succeeding. After analyzing current census data, CIS reports that legal and illegal immigration will reach an astounding 51 million in the next eight years, which represents 82 percent of the population growth in America, meaning that the immigrant population is growing four times faster than the native-born population. The Census Bureau projects the 2023 total immigrant population will reach 14.8 percent, the highest level ever reported.[66]

The American people are broadly opposed to these immigration policies. According to The Pew Research Center, 69 percent of Americans want to restrict and control immigration rates—72 percent of whites, 66 percent of blacks, and 59 percent of Hispanics.[67] Gallup reports that by two to one, Americans want immigration levels reduced[68]; and *Reuters* found that by nearly three to one, Americans want immigration levels reduced.[69]

The phrase *E Pluribus Unum*, "out of many, one," is part of the centerpiece of the Great Seal of the United States. It speaks to the unity of the states and the people, despite their diverse backgrounds, as one American identity with a distinctly American culture. The most troublesome aspect of unbridled immigration and hostility toward assimilation is the certainty with which it will disunite and unravel America—as millions of new immigrants self-segregate into ethnic, racial, and religious enclaves. It also clearly and hugely influences adversely the economy, employment, governmental spending, and more. And those who will suffer most are, yet again, younger people and future generations, who will inherit what has been wrought.

## SEVEN

## ON THE ENVIRONMENT

SO YOU THOUGHT THE environmental movement was about clean air, clean water, and polar bears? Such messages are especially seductive to younger people, albeit hugely deceptive and manipulative.

John Beale is a former top-ranking Environmental Protection Agency (EPA) official in the Obama administration who was sentenced to prison for fraud. But starting in mid-2009, he told congressional investigators he was working on a "green economics" project to "modify the DNA of the capitalist system." As reported by Fox News, "he argued that environmental regulation was reaching its 'limits' because 'the fundamental dynamic of the capitalistic system is for businesses and individuals to try to externalize costs.'"[1]

Beale is among a growing number of self-appointed statists, mostly unknown to the public, who have insinuated themselves into positions of governance or hold themselves out as experts, and whose real ideology and agenda extend far beyond clean air and water. For example, in a recent interview, fanatical anticapitalist and "climate activist" Naomi Klein proclaimed that "Capitalism increasingly is a discredited system because it is seen as a system that venerates greed above all else. . . . There's a benefit to climate discussion to name a system that lots of people already have problems with for other reasons." She continued, "I don't know why it is so important to save capitalism. It is a pretty battered brand. . . . Just focusing on climate is getting us nowhere. . . . Many, many more people recognize the need to change our economy. . . . If climate can be our lens to catalyze this economic transformation that so many people need for other even more pressing reasons then that may be a winning combination." Klein added, "This economic system is failing the vast majority of people. . . . [Capitalism] is also waging a war on the planet's life support system."[2]

Much of the so-called environmental movement today has transmuted into an aggressively nefarious and primitive faction. In the last fifteen years, many of the tenets of utopian statism have coalesced around something called the "degrowth" movement. Originating in Europe but now taking a firm hold in the United States, the "degrowthers," as I shall characterize them, include in their ranks none other than

President Barack Obama. On January 17, 2008, Obama made clear his hostility toward, of all things, electricity generated from coal and coal-powered plants. He told the *San Francisco Chronicle,* "You know, when I was asked earlier about the issue of coal . . . under my plan of a cap and trade system, electricity rates would necessarily skyrocket. . . ."[3] Obama added, ". . . So if somebody wants to build a coal-powered plant, they can. It's just that it will bankrupt them because they're going to be charged a huge sum for all the greenhouse gas that's being emitted."[4]

Degrowthers define their agenda as follows: "Sustainable degrowth is a downscaling of production and consumption that increases human well-being and enhances ecological conditions and equity on the planet. It calls for a future where societies live within their ecological means, with open localized economies and resources more equally distributed through new forms of democratic institutions."[5] It "is an essential economic strategy to pursue in overdeveloped countries like the United States—for the well-being of the planet, of underdeveloped populations, and yes, even of the sick, stressed, and overweight 'consumer' populations of overdeveloped countries."[6]

For its proponents and adherents, degrowth has quickly developed into a pseudo-religion and public-policy obsession. In fact, the degrowthers insist their ideology reaches far beyond the environment or even its odium for capitalism and is an all-encompassing lifestyle and governing philosophy. Some of its leading advocates argue that "Degrowth is not just an economic concept. We shall show that it is a frame constituted by a large array of concerns, goals, strategies and actions. As a result, degrowth has now become a confluence point where streams of critical ideas and political action converge."[7] Degrowth is "an interpretative frame for a social movement, understood as the mechanism through which actors engage in a collective action."[8]

The degrowthers seek to eliminate carbon sources of energy and redistribute wealth according to terms they consider equitable. They reject the traditional economic reality that acknowledges growth as improving living conditions generally but especially for the impoverished. They embrace the notions of "less competition, large scale redistribution, sharing and reduction of excessive incomes and wealth."[9] Degrowthers want to engage in polices that will set "a maximum income, or maximum wealth, to weaken envy as a motor of consumerism, and opening borders ("no-border") to reduce means to keep inequality between rich and poor countries."[10] And they demand reparations by supporting a "concept of ecological debt, or the demand that the Global North pays for past and present colonial exploitation in the Global South."[11]

French economist and leading degrowther Serge Latouche asserts that "We are currently witnessing the steady commercialization of everything in the world. Applied to every domain in this way, capitalism cannot help but destroy the planet much as it destroys society, since the very idea of the market depends on unlimited excess and domination."[12] He also abhors economic growth and wealth creation, the very attributes necessary to improve the human condition and societies: "A society based on economic contraction cannot exist under capitalism."[13] Indeed, on July 18, 2014, scores of extreme groups throughout the world endorsed a proclamation titled the *Margarita Declaration on Climate Change* ("changing the system not the climate"), which calls for, among other things, an end to the "capitalist hegemonic system."[14]

Degrowth is "usually characterized by a strong utopian dimension." Its foundations rely on a version of "economic relations based on sharing, gifts and reciprocity, where social relations and conviviality are central."[15]

To implement this utopian vision of radical egalitarian outcomes, the degrowth movement employs strategies such as "alternative building, opposition and research, and in relation to capitalism, they can be 'anti-capitalist,' 'post capitalist' and 'despite capitalism.'"[16] The degrowthers insist that governments establish a living wage and reduce the workweek to twenty hours.[17] Apparently discounting the fact that the population of the globe has increased by several billion human beings in the intervening years, they call for bringing "material production back down to the levels of the 1960s and 1970s" and "return[ing] to small-scale farming."[18] And degrowthers "[d]ecree a moratorium on technological innovation, pending an in-depth assessment of its achievements and a reorientation of scientific and technical research according to new aspirations."[19] Imagine the power and breadth of the police state necessary to enforce this form of antediluvian autocracy.

We need not look far. In 1848, in *The Communist Manifesto*, Karl Marx and Friedrich Engels declared, in part: "The bourgeoisie cannot exist without constantly revolutionizing the instruments of production, and thereby the relations of production, and with them the whole relations of society. . . . Constant revolutionizing of production, uninterrupted disturbance of all social conditions, everlasting uncertainty and agitation, distinguish the bourgeois epoch from all earlier ones. All fixed, fast-frozen relations, with their train of ancient and venerable prejudices and opinions, are swept away; all new-formed ones become antiquated before they can ossify. All that is solid melts into air, all that is holy is profaned, and man is at last compelled to face with sober senses his real conditions of life and his relations with his kind. The need of a constantly expanding market for its products chases the bourgeoisie over the whole surface of the globe. It must nestle everywhere, settle everywhere, establish connections everywhere."[20]

Over forty-years ago, philosopher and author Ayn Rand, in her book *Return of the Primitive—The Anti-Industrial Revolution*, wrote presciently that the statists had changed their line of attack. "Instead of their old promises that collectivism would create universal abundance and their denunciations of capitalism for creating poverty, they are now denouncing capitalism for creating abundance. Instead of promising comfort and security for everyone, they are now denouncing people for being comfortable and secure."[21] She continued: "The demand to 'restrict' technology is the demand to *restrict* man's mind. It is nature—i.e., reality—that makes both these goals impossible to achieve. Technology can be destroyed, and the mind can be paralyzed, but neither can be restricted. Whether and wherever such restrictions are attempted, it is the mind—not the state—that withers away."[22] "To restrict technology would require omniscience—a total knowledge of all the possible effects and consequences of a given development for all the potential innovators of the future. Short of such omniscience, restrictions mean the attempt to regulate the unknown, to limit the unborn, to set rules for the undiscovered."[23] "A stagnant technology is the equivalent of a stagnant mind. A 'restricted' technology is the equivalent of a *censored* mind."[24]

The degrowthers would deindustrialize advanced economies, destroy modernity, and turn plenty into scarcity. As utopian statists, or what I have characterized in the past as enviro-statists, degrowthers reject experience, knowledge, and science, for a paradisiacal abstraction, while claiming to have mastered them all. Ultimately, for the more fanatical among them, the ultimate purpose is revolution and transformation; the environment is incidental if not extraneous to their central mission, except as a cunning stratagem.

Most Americans do not wish to throw themselves into a regressive, primal lifestyle. They enjoy the abundance of untold human benefits and improvements resulting from entrepreneurship, capitalism, and economic growth. Consequently, the degrowth movement has attempted to conceal its pagan-like militant opposition to fossil fuels and carbon dioxide by mainstreaming its agenda with politically generated and well-funded campaigns promoting what was once called "man-made global cooling," then "man-made global warming," and now "man-made climate change." Nonetheless, like most dogmatists, the degrowthers are impatient. The revolution is now and change must be immediate. Thus, the degrowthers' agenda is built around hysterical doomsday predictions of environmental armageddon, which can only be avoided by the imposition of their severe, ideologically driven agenda.

Dr. Mark J. Perry, a scholar at the American Enterprise Institute (AEI) and a professor of economics and finance at the University of Michigan, compiled a list of "18 spectacularly wrong apocalyptic predictions made around the time of the first Earth Day in 1970," including the end of Western civilization in fifteen or thirty years; the end of the nation and the world as a suitable place for human habitation; and an increase in the death rate of at least 100 to 200 million people each year during the next ten years due to starvation. By 2000, most of the world will be in famine; by 1985, air pollution will reduce sunlight on earth, requiring city populations to wear gas masks; the rate of nitrogen in the atmosphere will be so significant that in time none of our land will be usable; two hundred thousand Americans will die in 1973 from smog disasters in New York and Los Angeles; before 1990, the world will run out of lead, zinc, tin, gold, and silver; by 2000, there will be no more crude oil; after 2000, the world will run out of copper; in twenty-five years between 75 and 80 percent of all species of animals will be extinct; and so on.[25]

In 2008, Dr. John Brignell, retired professor of industrial instrumentation at the University of Southampton in Britain, composed a list of more than five hundred alarmist claims made in news reports of damage supposedly caused by "man-made global warning," which are so utterly preposterous I was compelled to publish them in my book *Liberty and Tyranny*, but are too numerous to list here.[26]

In this milieu of statist-generated delirium, the degrowthers ensconced in the federal government are imposing on society infinite "ameliorative" rules, regulations, and coercive edicts, and the necessary fines, penalties, and even jail sentences to enforce them. And those who object to these governmental commands and challenge the "science" behind them are ridiculed and dismissed as, among other things, "climate-change deniers" or "flat-earthers."

In the last several years, particularly during the Obama administration, the federal government has embraced key elements of the degrowther movement and issued a rash of "major" regulations. Major regulations are rules that are likely to result in "(1) An annual effect on the economy of $100 million or more; (2) A major increase in costs or prices for consumers, individual industries, Federal, State, or local government agencies, or geographic regions; or (3) Significant adverse effects on competition, employment, investment, productivity, innovation, or on the ability of United States–based enterprises to compete with foreign-based enterprises in domestic or export markets."[27]

The EPA is the main federal governmental fortress for the degrowth agenda. Consistent with the ideological aims of the degrowth movement, the EPA has dedicated itself to gutting the production of carbon-based resources such as coal, oil, and natural gas as supplies of relatively cheap and abundant electricity and fuel. In recent years, the EPA has tenaciously ramped up its regulatory efforts to cripple the production of energy from these sources. Since 2010, the EPA has issued sixty-five major regulations affecting all manner of industries.[28] In 2014 alone, the EPA promulgated thirteen major regulations.[29] Affected industries include: energy companies (particularly coal companies); the auto industry; commercial and solid waste incinerators; portland cement manufacturing; oceangoing ships; petrochemical companies; the airline industry; the construction industry; and home builders and contractors.[30] In 2015, the EPA is completing twenty-five major regulations and plans on proposing twenty-six new major regulations.[31] Affected industries include, again, energy companies, the auto industry, and construction, as well as farming.[32] The Heritage Foundation concludes that by 2038, the carbon-dioxide rules alone, which phase out the use of coal, an abundant natural resource in the United States, will cost the nation nearly six hundred thousand jobs and an aggregate gross domestic product decrease of $2.23 trillion.[33]

Lest we forget, before the Industrial Revolution, for many centuries mankind's condition experienced little improvement. As University of California historian and economics professor Dr. Gregory Clark explains, "Life expectancy was no higher in 1800 than for hunter-gathers; thirty to thirty-five years. Stature, a measure of both the quality of diet and children's exposure to disease, was higher in the Stone Age than in 1800."[34] Even for the relatively wealthy, as recently as the eighteenth century life was very difficult. Moreover, the "modest comforts" of society in 1800 "were purchased only through a life of unrelenting drudgery."[35]

In America today, even poor families are much better off than is widely believed. This is not to say that they do not struggle or to downplay cases of significant hardship, but it is worth knowing the statistical facts, most of which are generated by the federal government. For example, a recent Heritage Foundation study found that despite media and other portrayals, including those of the degrowthers, acute and widespread hunger mostly does not exist in the United States. "The U.S. Department of Agriculture collects data on these topics in its household food security survey. For 2009, the survey showed: 96 percent of poor parents stated that their children were never hungry at any time during the year because they could not afford food; 83 percent of poor families reported having enough food to eat; 82 percent of poor adults reported never being hungry at any time in the prior year due to lack of money for food. Other government surveys show that the average consumption of protein, vitamins, and minerals is virtually the same for poor and middle-class children and is well above recommended norms in most cases."[36]

In addition, "[o]ver the course of a year, 4 percent of poor persons become temporarily homeless. Only 9.5 percent of the poor live in mobile homes or trailers, 49.5 percent live in separate single-family houses or townhouses, and 40 percent live in apartments. Forty-two percent of poor households actually own their own homes. Only 6 percent of poor households are overcrowded. More than two-thirds have more than two rooms per person. The vast majority of the homes or apartments of the poor are in good repair." It concluded that "[b]y their own reports, the average poor person had sufficient funds to meet all essential needs and to obtain medical care for family members throughout the year whenever needed."[37]

Infectious diseases and other illnesses have been rampant throughout human history. While many diseases still plague mankind, enormous advances have been made in treating or eliminating untold numbers of them. This progress did not magically occur from feel-good intentions and redistributionist policies. Although public health actions have contributed to this remarkable development, modern medicine owes its evolution, in significant part, to science made possible by abundant energy derived from carbon sources.

University of Chicago history professor Dr. Kenneth Pomeranz explains that the European technological breakthroughs of the Industrial Revolution are based appreciably on the abundance of coal as a viable natural resource. He states: "Thus it seems sensible, after all, to look at the mining and uses of coal as the most likely European technological advantage that was purely home-grown, crucial to its nineteenth-century breakthrough, and (unlike textiles) not dependent for its full flowering on European access to overseas resources."[38] By the year 1800, economists believe, humanity had reached the limits of development without the technological marvels of the Industrial Revolution. "All societies before 1800 had to produce resources—food, energy, raw materials—on a renewable basis from a fixed land area. The 'advanced organic technology' of Europe and Asia was at its natural limits by 1800."[39] The technological developments of the Industrial Revolution were not attainable without "plentiful coal and the easing of other resource constraints made possible by the New World."[40] For example, "Britain's coal output would increase fourteen times from 1815 to 1900, but its sugar imports increased roughly eleven-fold over the same period, and its cotton imports increased a stunning twenty-fold."[41] Therefore, economists conclude, "Europe made [the] leap because it had coal reserves readily accessible to its population centers."[42] Furthermore, it had "the massive largely empty land area of the Americas relatively close at hand, to lift for a time the ecological constraint with a continent-sized flood of food and raw materials."[43]

Coal, an abundant and efficient resource, in combination with the modern market-based capitalist system, clearly benefited poorer people more than other groups. Dr. Pomeranz continues: "[U]nskilled labor has reaped more gains than any other group. Marx and Engels, trumpeting their gloomy prognostications in *The Communist Manifesto* . . . could not have been more wrong about the fate of unskilled workers."[44] Beginning in 1815, "real wages in England for both farm laborers and the urban unskilled had begun the inexorable rise that has created affluence for all."[45]

Dr. Clark also points out that women in particular benefited from the Industrial Revolution. "Rising incomes switched the emphasis of production away from sectors such as agriculture (which demanded strength) toward such sectors as manufacturing and service (in which dexterity was more important)."[46]

The examples of capitalism generating human and societal improvement are infinite. As I explained in *Liberty and Tyranny*: "[S]cientific and technological advances, especially since the Industrial Revolution, have hugely benefited mankind. Running water and indoor plumbing enable fresh water to be brought into the home and dirty water to be removed through a system of aqueducts, wells, dams, and sewage treatment facilities; irrigating and fertilizing land creates more stable and plentiful food supplies; harnessing natural resources such as coal, oil, and gas make possible the delivery of power to homes, hospitals, schools, and businesses and fuel for automobiles, trucks, and airplanes; networks of paved roads promote mobility, commerce, and assimilation; and the invention of medical devices and discovery of chemical substances extend and improve the quality of life."[47]

Plants cannot exist without carbon dioxide. And through a natural process called photosynthesis, they convert carbon dioxide into oxygen. Carbon dioxide has never been a pollutant. Furthermore, it is not covered under the Clean Air Act. Indeed, carbon dioxide makes up a minuscule fraction of greenhouse gases (water vapor is the most significant element), and greenhouse gases make up no more than about 2 percent of the entire atmosphere.[48] Yet, without greenhouse gases, including carbon dioxide, temperatures would drop so low that the planet would freeze, oceans would turn into ice, and life would cease to exist. Dr. Patrick Moore, a top ecologist and cofounder of Greenpeace, is among many experts who have insisted that "There is no scientific proof that human emissions of carbon dioxide are the dominant cause of the minor warming of the Earth's atmosphere over the past 100 years. If there were such proof it would be written down for all to see. No actual proof, as it is understood in science, exists."[49] Dr. Moore is not alone. Some thirty thousand other experts agree with him.[50]

No matter, the EPA zealously and relentlessly abuses and exceeds its regulatory authority, delegated by Congress under the Clean Air Act (enacted by Congress in the 1970s and amended in the 1990s), which was originally intended to limit the emissions of actual pollutants. It repeatedly usurps the law, having been provided cover by the U.S. Supreme Court for unleashing numerous and onerous rules intended to wipe out entire industries that provide safe and reliable energy to millions of homes and businesses.[51]

Consequently, in 2013, 2014, and 2015, the EPA released (or is planning to release) a series of regulations designed to destroy the coal industry and diminish the oil and gas industries. The first of these rules, the "New Source Performance Rule" (NSPS), mandates that every newly constructed coal-burning power plant in the United States use a costly and unproven technology to reduce its carbon emissions.[52] The cost of implementing this technology is so exorbitant it makes building most new, coal-burning power plants impracticable. There is currently only one coal-burning power plant under construction in the United States. Its erection has been stymied by exorbitant cost overruns and delays.[53]

The second of these regulations, the "Existing Source Performance Rule" (ESPR), sets preposterously high emission standards for power plants, including those that burn coal.[54] The goal of this rule is to force current power plants that use carbon sources such as coal and natural gas to charge increasingly higher rates to consumers for power, eventually driving these energy companies out of business.

The harsh consequences of these sorts of regulations are evident in Canada, where the residents of Ontario have experienced huge increases in power costs. The *Financial Post* reports that "The cost of electricity for the average Ontario consumer went from $780 [to] more than $1,800, with more increases to come." This increase occurred because the controlling political party replaced "fossil-fuel generated electricity with renewable energy from wind, solar and biomass."[55] Reliance on renewable energy, however, raised a new set of problems. "Billions more were needed for transmission lines to hook up the new wind and solar generators. At the same time, wind and solar generation—being unstable—needed back-up generation, which forced the construction of new gas plants." The construction of new plants led to a government boondoggle. "The gas plants themselves became the target of further government intervention, leading to the $1 billion gas plant scandal."[56]

And the third of these regulations, "the Green Power Plan," targets oil and gas production, including hydraulic fracturing or "fracking," which uses technological advances to extract natural gas from shale rock layers by imposing severe limits on methane emissions.[57] Methane is an even smaller greenhouse gas element than carbon dioxide. At a time when the United States is on the verge of realizing the half-century-old goal of energy independence, the EPA is actively suffocating the industries, innovations, and technologies responsible for the progress. And it is doing so despite the fact that its own recent study found "no evidence that these mechanisms have led to widespread, systemic impacts on drinking water resources in the United States."[58]

The EPA's rules are only the latest steps in an endless staircase of planned governmental actions intended to phase out carbon as an energy source, institute by coercion major parts of the degrowth agenda through deindustrialization, drive up the cost of energy production and use, and ultimately drive down the quality of life and living standards of Americans—who are supposedly fouling the earth with their capitalist extravagances. In fact, the degrowthers refer to this effort as "Energy Descent Action Plans." These plans are part of a broader social-engineering project known as "Transition."[59] And Transition is only one of many action plans for degrowth involving "pricing carbon out of the economy," "shifting from an energy-obese to an energy-healthy society," "establishing a 'New Green Deal,'" and "rapidly relocalising the economy."[60]

Of course, if the plan is to unravel and remake the existing society and economy, the degrowthers must not limit their demands, plans, and interventions merely to energy production and use. And they are not. For example, through the EPA, the degrowthers are abusing and expanding its authority under another federal law, this time the Clean Water Act of 1972.[61] Under the Constitution, Congress has the power to regulate only interstate commerce and only waterways that could be used as commercial channels of navigation across state boundaries. The act's language specifically acknowledges that the states regulate bodies of water within their boundaries, insisting that Congress will continue to "recognize, preserve and protect the primary responsibilities of the states."[62] But the EPA brazenly issued a rule seizing the authority to regulate virtually any body of water that—no matter how intermittently—flows into a stream or tributary, and in so doing inflated the definition of "navigable waterways."[63] This regulation obligates any property owner, including farmers, ranchers, and homeowners, to expend untold sums of money obtaining permits from the federal government before taking any action that might conceivably—no matter how unlikely such a result is—affect ponds, lakes, or streams on their own property.

Clearly the degrowth movement is not about reasonable conservation efforts, minimizing pollution through practicable policies, or averting the gratuitous destruction of natural habitats and ecosystems. As Rand wrote, the truth is that the first targets and victims of the enviro-statists and their degrowth crusade are the "young, ambitious and poor." "The young people who work their way through college; the young couples who plan their future, budgeting their money and their time; the young men and women who aim at a career; the struggling artists, writers, composers who have to earn a living, while developing their creative talents; any purposeful human-being—i.e., the best of mankind. To them, *time* is the one priceless commodity, most passionately needed. *They* are the main beneficiaries of electric percolators, frozen food, washing machines, and labor-saving devices. And if the production and, above all, the *invention* of such devices is retarded or diminished by the ecological crusade, it will be one of the darkest crimes against humanity—particularly because the victims' agony will be private, their voices will not be heard, and their absence will not be noticed publicly until a generation or two later (by which time, the survivors will not be able to notice anything)."[64]

EIGHT

## ON THE MINIMUM WAGE

THE MINIMUM WAGE, AND constant demands for its increase, is said to be compassionate. But the concrete evidence
shows it is a job killer, especially for low- or unskilled workers
in general, and younger people in particular.

The number of long-term unemployed (those jobless for
twenty-seven weeks or more) stood at 2.6 million as of March
2015.[1] The number of individuals employed in part-time work
for "economic reasons" (those individuals who are not part-
time workers by choice, or "involuntary part-time workers")
was 6.7 million in March 2015.[2] From a historical perspective,
the number of involuntary part-time workers is particularly
high. In 1990, for example, there were approximately 4.8 million individuals who were considered "involuntary part-time

workers."[3] A recent poll of the unemployed, completed in May 2014, revealed that 47 percent have "completely given up" looking for a job.[4]

The labor force participation rate—the percentage of the population age sixteen and over employed for March 2015— stood at 62.7 percent.[5] For comparison, the labor force participation rate in 1990 was 66.8 percent.[6] The labor force participation rate reflects the percentage of individuals who are actually working and paying taxes. The unemployment rate, by contrast, reflects the percentage of individuals who are actively searching for jobs—not those individuals who have given up searching for employment. The federal government defines unemployment as "people who are jobless, looking for jobs, and available for work."[7]

According to an analysis conducted by the Senate Budget Committee, as of September 26, 2014, nearly one in four Americans between the ages of twenty-five and fifty-four was not working. In absolute numbers, this translates to 28.9 million Americans between these ages who are not working versus 95.6 million who are working.[8]

There are a number of explanations for why the labor force in the United States is shrinking. First, the American population is aging. As the largest population cohort, the ruling generation is getting older and retiring. And a larger percentage of the population is physically incapable of work. Second, as indicated in the recent poll of long-term unemployed, many of those who do not have jobs have stopped looking for work.

Discouraged by employment prospects, these individuals have simply dropped out of the labor force despite having a desire and the capacity to hold a job. A shrinking labor force is particularly problematic for the rising generation. Instead of the older generation retiring and subsequent generations filling jobs behind them, jobs are disappearing. Businesses are making the decision not to hire new workers. Fewer available jobs equates to less actual employment. Moreover, as described in chapter 6, unprecedented waves of immigration, legal and illegal, drive down employment opportunities for American citizens, particularly younger people, as does the government's degrowth agenda, as described in chapter 7.

For teenagers, the March 2015 unemployment rate stood at 17.5 percent.[9] For the general population, the unemployment rate for whites was 4.7 percent; for African Americans, 10.1 percent; and for Hispanics, 6.8 percent.[10] Furthermore, younger people are in a much worse position than their parents and grandparents. A survey completed by CareerBuilder indicated that "[w]hile the number of jobs held by [individuals aged 55–64] grew by 9 percent from 2007 to 2013, jobs held by [individuals aged 25–34] have increased a mere .3 percent."[11] In actual terms, those numbers "translate to a gain of 1.9 million jobs versus 110,000 jobs, respectively."[12]

In March 2015, there were approximately 2.1 million individuals who "were marginally attached to the labor force."[13] This means an individual is not employed, wants to find employment, and searched for a job in the past twelve months.

These individuals are considered "marginally attached" because they have not searched for a job "in the 4 weeks preceding the [employment] survey."[14]

Obtaining an entry-level job for teenagers and young adults is a necessary aspect of becoming an adult. Gainful employment inculcates responsibility and a sense of self-worth. It also allows those individuals to supplement the household income—if necessary, helping to support the family. However, obtaining a job for many young people is extremely difficult.

According to President Barack Obama, increasing the amount federal contractors pay their employees to a minimum of $10.10 an hour (up from the $7.25 minimum hourly wage) "would lift millions of Americans out of poverty immediately. It would help millions more work their way out of poverty—without requiring a single dollar in new taxes or spending."[15] Always quick to demonize the opposition, Obama characterized those who disagreed with his position as "out of step and [putting] politics ahead of working Americans."[16] He insisted that a minimum wage "means making sure workers have the chance to save for a dignified retirement."[17] But forcing employers to pay more for unskilled or less-skilled workers, many of whom are younger, on top of the other statist economic and social policies, discourages employee retention and hiring.

Consider some basic economic truths. If the government mandates that workers who are earning $7.25 must, overnight, be paid $10.10 an hour (or even $15.00 per hour) those new dollars must originate from some source. For example, if a fast-food restaurant that employs twenty individuals is required to pay some or all of them close to 30 percent more per hour, it must account for those dollars somewhere. The restaurant can try to sell more food, it can increase the cost of food, it can cut the hours of its employees, it can hire fewer workers, or it can lay off those currently employed.

In addition, increasing the minimum wage directly and adversely affects youth employment because younger people are most likely to seek low-skilled jobs.[18] For many teenagers, their employment experience begins at the local fast-food restaurant, bowling alley, or department store. Therefore, any mandate from the government that employers pay an established wage reduces opportunities for America's youth to obtain entry-level jobs.[19] The supply and demand for professional jobs requiring medical, law, or engineering degrees are not adversely affected by an increase in the minimum wage. They require specialized skills, and those skills translate to higher wages. Low-skilled and unskilled lower-end jobs, often filled by younger people and first-time employees, are the most at risk when the government raises the minimum wage.

In the United States, the concept of a "minimum wage" arose from policies advanced by the Progressive Movement in the early twentieth century.[20] Initially conceived as a floor for wages paid to employees, the first iterations of minimum wage laws applied to women and children in the labor force.[21] Established in the states, the first of these laws applied to specific industries such as garment workers. Utah was the first state to

set a flat-rate floor for wages that applied to all industries.[22]
These laws, however, were quickly challenged by business
owners and, in 1923, the U.S. Supreme Court declared them
unconstitutional.

In *Adkins* v. *Children's Hospital*, the Court found the District of Columbia's minimum wage law unconstitutional. It
ruled that a minimum wage law improperly interfered with the
due process clause's protections pertaining to the freedom to
enter into contracts. Specifically, the law unduly impeded the
individual's right to contract:

> [T]wo parties having lawful capacity—under penalties as
> to the employer—to freely contract with one another in
> respect of the price for which one shall render service to
> the other in a purely private employment where both are
> willing, perhaps anxious, to agree, even though the consequence may be to oblige one to surrender a desirable
> engagement and the other to dispense with the services
> of a desirable employee.[23]

As a result of this decision, many of the early minimum
wage laws atrophied. One study conducted in 1991 determined that by the end of the 1920s "seven of the original seventeen minimum wage laws were declared unconstitutional,
five others were either repealed or not enforced."[24]

With the onset of the Great Depression and the advent
of the New Deal, there was a renewed movement to establish

a federal minimum wage applicable to all industries. Shortly after his re-election in 1936, President Franklin Roosevelt engaged in a public effort to improperly influence the Supreme Court. The Court's earlier decisions declaring aspects of Roosevelt's New Deal unconstitutional raised his ire. He threatened to pack the Court with individuals who shared his political and policy views. Though he never carried out his threats, as even members of his own party in Congress objected, Roosevelt's intimidation had the desired effect. In 1937, the Court reversed its position on the minimum wage by upholding the state of Washington's minimum wage law.[25]

After this change of course, and at Roosevelt's urging, Congress enacted the Fair Labor Standards Act (FLSA) establishing a minimum wage of twenty-five cents.[26] The law applied to "employees who produced products shipping in interstate commerce."[27] This provision was a transparent attempt to assuage the constitutional concerns regarding the infringement on private business arrangements between two parties—the suggestion being that Congress has the power to regulate commerce between and among states. Minimum wage laws are now seen everywhere, and politicians at the federal, state, and local levels of government are constantly pressing to increase these minimums.

Instead of alleviating poverty and generating employment, the FLSA's minimum wage provisions actually extended the Great Depression. Economists Harold L. Cole and Lee E. Ohanian found that "high wages reduced employment directly in the cartelized sectors of the economy, and also reduced employment in the non-cartelized sectors through general equilibrium effects."[28] They concluded "that the recovery from the Depression would have been much stronger if these policies had not been adopted."[29] As such, mandating a minimum wage eliminated a commonsense approach available to employers when experiencing an economic downturn: broadly reducing all wages to avoid firing employees. In lieu of reducing wages, employers were forced to lay off workers or avoid hiring new workers or both. As Cole and Ohanian point out, this affected not only the specific industries subject to regulation under the FLSA, but the entire economy, thereby helping to prolong the Great Depression.

Nonetheless, the federal government alone has raised the federal minimum wage twenty-two times since its inception. The minimum wage is currently $7.25 per hour, and there are widespread efforts to increase this amount to $10.10.[30] In 2013, the BLS reports, there were 79.5 million workers age sixteen and older who were paid by the hour—this accounts for 58.8 percent of all workers. Some 1.5 million workers earned the federal minimum wage ($7.25 per hour).[31] Although those earning the federal minimum wage represent a small percentage of the total workforce, the younger the worker the more likely his employment status is to be harmed by the minimum wage.

It is important to emphasize that most workers who are paid the minimum wage are young. Workers under age twenty-five compose approximately 20 percent of the total workforce, but they make up approximately half of those who earn the federal minimum wage.[32] About 20 percent of employed teenagers earn the minimum wage, compared with 3 percent of workers over the age of twenty-five.[33] Moreover, approximately 10 percent of part-time workers and approximately 2 percent of full-time workers earn the minimum wage.[34]

Even so, Obama, among others, creates the impression that those who earn the minimum wage are largely heads of households and sole providers for their families. The minimum wage is said to be a lifeline keeping millions off the breadlines. In a signing ceremony touting his executive order directing federal contractors to raise the minimum wage, Obama surrounded himself with older workers who earn the minimum wage when he made his announcement. He stated, "I've invited some of the folks who would see a raise if we raised the minimum wage. . . . And like most workers in their situation, they're not teenagers. . . . They're adults—average age is 35 years old." He continued, "Many of them have children that they're supporting. These are Americans who work full-time, often to support a family, and if the minimum wage had kept pace with our economic productivity, they'd already be getting paid well over $10 an hour."[35]

According to Obama, a failure of Congress to raise the minimum wage amounts to a consignment to poverty. "[T]he failure of Congress to act was the equivalent of a $200 pay cut. . . . That's a month worth of groceries, maybe two months'

worth of electricity. It makes a big difference for a lot of families."[36] Of course, he utters not a word about the untold number of younger people who would lose their jobs or be priced
out of the entry-level job market.

The effects of the imposition of a minimum wage on the
economy have been evaluated by economists using different
types of models. (The term "model" refers to a method for
applying and analyzing given data.) First among these models
is the basic competitive (or neoclassical) model, which demonstrates that when the government establishes a minimum
wage above the market-driven wage, it increases a business's
cost of production and induces two economy-wide effects.[37] In
their book *Minimum Wages*, University of California economics professor Dr. David Neumark and Federal Reserve policy
expert William L. Wascher explain that "First, the price of the
output rises and the demand for it falls, leading to a decline
in production (the 'scale effect')." Next, "the higher wage rate
causes [businesses] to substitute capital for labor in the production process (the 'substitution effect'). As a result, the demand
for labor falls."[38] This negative demand for labor "applies un-
ambiguously only to less-skilled workers whose wages are directly raised by the minimum wage."[39] In other words, under
the basic competitive model, the cost of the output (whether
it is hamburgers or candy at the drugstore) increases. And unskilled and low-skilled jobs are lost when the minimum wage
is increased.

As should be clear by now, businesses make adjustments

when the minimum wage is increased. Cato Institute scholar Mark Wilson explains that "all economists agree that businesses will make changes to adapt to the higher labor costs after a minimum wage increase." "The higher costs will be passed on to someone in the long run; the only question is who."[40]

Consider the case of SeaTac, a suburb of Seattle that increased its minimum wage for certain service industry employees to fifteen dollars per hour starting January 1, 2014. The *Seattle Times* reported in February 2014: "At the Clarion Hotel off International Boulevard, a sit-down restaurant has been shuttered, though it might be replaced by a less-labor-intensive café. . . . Other businesses have adjusted in ways that run the gamut from putting more work in the hands of managers, to instituting a small 'living-wage surcharge' for a daily parking space near the airport." Some businesses in SeaTac have cut benefits to their employees. When asked whether they appreciated the increase in the minimum wage, a hotel employee replied, "I lost my 401k, health insurance, paid holiday and vacation." The hotel reportedly offered meals to its employees. Now the employees must bring their own food. The hotel has also cut overtime and the opportunity to earn overtime pay. A part-time waitress stated, "I've got $15 an hour, but all my tips are now much less."[41]

Economists Neumark and Wascher evaluated decades of studies analyzing the efficacy of the minimum wage and the various models used to analyze their economic effects. They concluded that "Based on the evidence from our nearly two decades of research on minimum wages, coupled with the evidence accumulated from an impressive body of research conducted by others, we find it very difficult to see a good economic rationale for continuing to seek a higher minimum wage."[42] Numerous economic studies conducted over decades are "fairly unambiguous—minimum wages reduce employment of low skilled workers." These "adverse effects [are] even more apparent when [the] research focuses on those directly affected by minimum wages."[43]

Furthermore, wages for low-skilled jobs are dictated by supply and demand, not "the unconstrained wage offers of employers."[44] "[W]e are hard-pressed to imagine a compelling argument for a higher minimum wage when it neither helps low-income families nor reduces poverty."[45] Neumark and Wascher cite a study that found the average wage for day laborers in California—a job completely unregulated and requiring minimal skills—is more than eleven dollars per hour.[46] In this case, the market and the laws of supply and demand increased hourly wages well above the current federal minimum wage.

A recent study by the Congressional Budget Office (CBO) underscores the findings of Neumark and Wascher. After examining the effects of raising the minimum wage, the CBO concludes that for those who keep their jobs, wages would obviously increase, however, "jobs for low-wage workers would probably be eliminated, the income of most workers who became jobless would fall substantially, and the share of low-wage workers who were employed would probably fall slightly."[47] Indeed, increasing the minimum wage would "reduce total employment by 500,000 workers." Moreover, most of the increased earnings of those who retain their jobs would not go to families below the poverty level because "many low-wage workers are not members of low-income families." The CBO estimates that of the $31 billion in increased earnings, 19 percent would go to households below the poverty line while 29 percent would go to families "earning more than three times the poverty threshold."[48]

It should now be obvious that the rising generation, particularly teenagers and young adults, is most adversely harmed by increases in the minimum wage, the consequences of which include pervasive unemployment and the lack of important job experience, affecting their future employment prospects and potential for success.

# NINE

---

# ON NATIONAL SECURITY

THE RISING GENERATION WILL suffer the most egregious afflictions and casualties should the governing generation and public officials fail to competently and adequately carry out their national security, military, and foreign policy duties. However, too many younger people are inattentive to or non-plussed about—or in rancorous opposition to—the development and maintenance of such policies. The rising generation has a responsibility to itself and future generations to properly comprehend the nature of the multiple national security threats America confronts.

The United States faces very serious national security threats from numerous sources including Islamic terrorism, which is spreading rapidly throughout the world and seeks to establish "sleeper cells" within America's borders; Communist China's extensive military build-up and expansionist designs; and fascist Russia's intimidation and invasion of sovereign neighbors. Moreover, North Korea, led by an erratic and menacing dictator, continually threatens nuclear and conventional war against American allies in the region; and Iran is a terrorist regime hell-bent on acquiring nuclear weapons. In addition, there are unstable nations that hold poorly secured nuclear weapons and even stockpiles that are sought by other regimes. No group of citizens should be more focused and diligent about America's national security and military readiness and deterrence capabilities than the members of the rising generation, inasmuch as younger people fight the country's wars.

National security threats have evolved speedily and dramatically during the last few decades. Traditional threats are posed to interests on land, sea, and in air. Modern threats have expanded to space and cyberspace. These "global commons" must also be protected in order to preserve America's security and economic interests.

In the late 1980s, the Soviet Union posed the greatest threat to the United States.[1] The Soviets amassed a powerful military, including nuclear weapon stocks. It had extensive international influence and an aggressive expansionist strategy.[2] However, as a result of the military, foreign, and economic policies instituted by President Ronald Reagan, in December 1991 the Soviet Union collapsed and a new era ushered in a different set of national security challenges.[3] Later, with the emergence of ex-KGB official and strongman Vladimir Putin as, effectively, Russia's dictator, Russia has followed a course of regional thuggery and military aggression, posing a renewed threat to the United States and its allies.

For example, in 2009, Russia effectively annexed the Georgian provinces of South Ossetia and Abkhazia.[4] In 2014, Russia annexed Crimea, sponsored armed rebellion and a separatist movement in eastern Ukraine, and escalated tensions with North Atlantic Treaty Organization (NATO) member nations in the region.[5] NATO now considers Russia its greatest threat.[6] According to a European Leadership Network report, "[t]hese events form a highly disturbing picture of violations of national airspace, emergency scrambles, narrowly avoided mid-air collisions, close encounters at sea, and other dangerous actions happening on a regular basis over a very wide geographical area."[7] In addition to these incidents, Russia has initiated military brushes near both the Canadian and American borders.[8]

China has embarked on a vigorous military and economic program designed to spread its influence regionally and worldwide.[9] From its bordering neighbors and the African continent to South and Central America, China is investing tens of billions of dollars in nation-building efforts obviously designed to increase its—and decrease American—influence.[10] China is also the principal supporter of oppressive regimes in North

Korea,[11] Syria,[12] and Venezuela.[13] And China is among the countries that have provided Iran with vital assistance in the development of its nuclear program.[14]

Furthermore, China seeks superiority in the East and South China Seas, where 90 percent of all global trade transits. China is building islands in the South China Sea, from where it is claiming territorial rights in international waters.[15] Defense and national security expert Tara Murphy notes that China is asserting exclusionary rights to waterways well beyond established international standards, which threatens to block trade access and could encourage other countries to institute similar polices.[16] Since 1996, China has prioritized the development of a naval fleet that will rival the United States Navy.[17] According to a United States Navy intelligence analysis, China's submarine capabilities have been greatly improved to the point where China is now able to launch long-range ballistic missiles that can reach America.[18] Alarmingly, senior navy intelligence officer Jesse Korotkin has determined that China is well ahead of schedule in its goal of modernizing its navy by 2020.[19] It has transitioned from a coastal defense navy to one capable of conducting multiple operations in nearly any part of the world.[20] China's current capabilities have the potential to cripple United States military operations from Guam to Okinawa, which would have a debilitating effect on America's defenses in the event of armed conflict.[21]

The Islamic regime in Iran is developing capabilities to strike American forces in the Persian Gulf.[22] More than 90 percent of Persian Gulf oil passes through the Strait of Hormuz, which borders Iran and is only twenty-one miles wide through its narrowest stretch.[23] Iran has significant mine-laying capabilities that threaten commercial and military vessels.[24] Iran also has a fleet of small but effective submarines, attack boats, and coastal missile batteries that can reach Israel.[25] Moreover, the 2013 Worldwide Threat Assessment of the United States Intelligence Community, released on January 24, 2014, warns that "Tehran has made technical progress in a number of areas—including uranium enrichment, nuclear reactors, and ballistic missiles—from which it could draw if it decided to build missile-deliverable nuclear weapons. These technical advancements strengthen our assessment that Iran has the scientific, technical, and industrial capacity to eventually produce nuclear weapons."[26] Director of National Intelligence James R. Clapper's assessment also cautions that "Iran would choose a ballistic missile as its preferred method of delivering nuclear weapons. Iran's ballistic missiles are inherently capable of delivering WMD, and Iran already has the largest inventory of ballistic missiles in the Middle East. Iran's progress on space launched vehicles—along with its desire to deter the United States and its allies—provides Iran with the means and motivation to develop longer range missiles, including intercontinental ballistic missiles (ICBM)."[27]

Incredibly, in the most recent Worldwide Threat Assessment of the U.S. Intelligence Community, released on February 26, 2015, for political reasons the Obama administration downplayed Iran's national security threat and does not even mention Iran in the section on terrorism, essentially white-washing Iran's significantly increased territorial gains and military advances.[28] However, Iran's designs on the Middle East and beyond are vast and growing. It is building "an arc of power" or "Shia crescent" stretching from Lebanon to Syria, Iraq to Yemen, and throughout other countries and territories by funding and arming terrorist surrogates.[29]

Respecting North Korea, the 2013 Worldwide Threat Assessment of the U.S. Intelligence Community report is alarming. It provides, in part, that "North Korea's nuclear weapons and missile programs pose a serious threat to the United States and to the security environment in East Asia, a region with some of the world's largest populations, militaries, and economies. North Korea's export of ballistic missiles to and associated materials to several countries, including Iran and Syria . . . illustrate the reach of its proliferation activities."[30] Indeed, as the *Wall Street Journal* recently reported, even the "latest Chinese estimates, relayed in a closed-door meeting with U.S. nuclear specialists, showed that North Korea may already have 20 warheads, as well as the capability of producing enough weapons-grade uranium to double its arsenal by next year, according to people briefed on the matter."[31]

More broadly, the 2013 Threat Assessment declares that "Nation-state efforts to develop or acquire weapons of mass destruction (WMD) and their delivery systems constitute a major threat to the security of our nation, deployed troops, and allies. The Intelligence Community is focused on the threat and destabilizing effects of nuclear proliferation, proliferation of chemical and biological warfare (CBW)-related materials, and development of WMD delivery systems."[32]

But over the last several decades, another kind of grave threat has emerged. In January 1987, the National Security Strategy of the United States declared, "An additional threat, which is particularly insidious in nature and growing in scope, is international terrorism—a worldwide phenomenon that is becoming increasingly frequent, indiscriminate, and state-sponsored."[33]

Beyond its military threat, Iran (in partnership with the Hezbollah terrorist organization) and other countries, such as Syria, Yemen, Lebanon, Libya, Tunisia, Afghanistan, Pakistan, Kazakhstan, Somalia, and others, sponsor, tolerate, or ineffectively oppose terrorist organizations training or operating within their borders.[34] Moreover, vast areas of the Middle East, Arabian Peninsula, and Sub-Saharan Africa are in turmoil.[35] And terrorist groups are taking advantage of the opportunities to fill the resulting power vacuum.[36]

In addition to state actors, there are the well-organized and well-financed terrorist organizations conquering vast land areas, where they are perpetrating heinous acts of inhumanity. Two of the most obvious examples are al-Qaeda and the Islamic State. They are dedicated to forming a "caliphate"—an Islamic government said to be led by the political and religious successor to the prophet Muhammad. Both are dedicated to the destruction of Western civilization. The national security implications for the United States and allies such as Israel, Egypt, Jordan, and Saudi Arabia, among others, are extremely dangerous.[37]

Al-Qaeda's stated goals are to "establish the rule of God on earth; attain martyrdom in the cause of God; and purification of the ranks of Islam from the elements of depravity."[38] The Islamic State seeks to establish the caliphate in Persia, first by taking over Iran in order to obtain Iran's nuclear weapons.[39]

The genocidal methods and aims of these terrorist groups cannot be overstated. The Islamic State urges the use of biological weapons on "unbelievers." A "fatwa" issued by an Islamic State cleric declares that "If Muslims cannot defeat the *kafir* [unbelievers] in a different way, it is permissible to use weapons of mass destruction."[40] Found on a laptop computer recovered from an Islamic State stronghold, the fatwa went on to justify the use weapons of mass destruction "[e]ven if it kills all of [the unbelievers] and wipes them and their descendants off the face of the earth."[41] Biological weapons are favored for terrorist use because they do not cost much money and can cause "huge" human casualties.[42] In a "how to" document also found on the Islamic State laptop, jihadists are encouraged to "use small grenades loaded with viruses" such as bubonic plague and to "throw them in closed areas like metros, soccer stadiums, or entertainment centers. But to do it next to the air conditioning."[43] Of course, these bombs "can also be used during suicide operations."[44]

The large-scale war crimes, crimes against humanity, and genocide perpetrated by the Islamic State terrorists and other jihadist groups remind the world daily of their calamitous threat to civilization and mankind.[45]

But terrorists are not living and training only in faraway Third World countries. Attacks have occurred in Paris, London, Madrid, and Jerusalem, and, obviously, in New York, Washington, and the skies above the United States on September 11, 2001, when nineteen al-Qaeda terrorists murdered thousands of Americans. It is also a virtual certainty that terrorist "sleeper cells" are secreted in America. In 2009, former director of national intelligence Dennis C. Blair warned Congress that terrorist organizations, including al-Qaeda and the Islamic State, are known to be working to radicalize Muslims in America.[46] Iran and Hezbollah have a strong recruiting presence in the United States, Mexico, and throughout Latin America.[47] Former Obama administration attorney general Eric Holder and California senator Dianne Feinstein, ranking Democrat on the Senate Intelligence Committee, acknowledged as much following the slaughter of writers and cartoonists at a Paris magazine office.[48] New America Foundation senior fellow Robert Wright explained that homegrown terrorists are an immediate concern, having already struck in the United States, for example, in the Fort Hood mass murder, which killed thirteen people, and the Boston Marathon bombing, which killed three and wounded more than 250.[49]

In February 2015, the same day federal authorities in New York charged three Muslim immigrants with conspiracy to provide material support to the Islamic State, FBI director James Comey told a meeting of state attorneys general: "I have home-grown violent extremist [domestic terrorist] investigations in every single state."[50] In April 2015, the United States attorney for Minnesota, Andrew Luger, announced that six Somali-American men from Minnesota, all naturalized American citizens, were charged with planning to join the Islamic State and that they were part of a larger conspiracy that included friends and relatives. He further declared: "We have a terror recruiting problem in Minnesota."[51]

A recent Pew Research Center analysis further underscores the seriousness of the problem.[52] The results of Pew's research discloses that while the vast majority of American Muslims oppose terrorist organizations and tactics, there are still a distressing number who support the use of terror tactics against civilians.[53]

Respondents were asked whether they believed that "suicide bombing or other forms of violence against civilian targets are justified to defend Islam from its enemies." While 81 percent oppose such tactics under any circumstances, 8 percent say these tactics are often or sometimes justified.[54] Another 5 percent responded that the use of violence against civilians might be justified in rare circumstances.[55] As there are 1.8 million adult American Muslims in the United States, this suggests that at least theoretically as many as thirteen thousand support the use of suicide bombs or other forms of terrorism. The survey also showed that native-born Muslims—in particular African-American Muslims—are more likely to support the use of violence.[56]

Pew reports that a "significant minority (21 percent) of Muslim Americans say that there is a great deal (6 percent) or a fair amount (15 percent) of support for extremism in the Muslim American community" and it is on the rise.[57] Furthermore, nearly half of American Muslims say that Muslim leaders in the United States are not doing enough to speak out against Islamic extremism.[58]

There are also significant technological threats to the nation's interests in space and cyberspace, which target nearly every American, the economy, and the country's security. For example, satellites have revolutionized communication throughout the world.[59] They are now critical to both commercial and military interests.[60] But satellites are vulnerable to destruction in two distinct ways—accidental collision and intentional interference or destruction.[61] China, Brazil, Iran, Iraq, and Turkey all have interfered with American satellite operations at one time or another in recent years.[62] China and Russia both have extensive space programs and are capable of significantly disrupting satellite security.[63]

The federal government, the military in particular, is dependent on the Internet and digital networks, making network infrastructure and security a significant vulnerability.[64] The Department of Defense (DOD) alone uses fifteen thousand networks and has 7 million computing devices in service, which has led the DOD to "formally recognize cyberspace for what it is—a domain similar to land, sea, air and space," according to former deputy secretary of defense William Lynn.[65] Lynn also noted that more than one hundred foreign intelligence agencies have tried to access American networks.[66]

According to a Pew Research Center study, 61 percent of cybersecurity experts believe that there will be a major cyberattack by 2025, which could result in severe economic losses and potentially significant loss of life.[67] The experts surveyed raised concerns about the vulnerability of the nation's financial system, power grid, air traffic control system, health-care system, and many other critical aspects of American society.[68]

In the meantime, Chinese hackers recently launched a massive attack on federal government databases, stealing personnel information and security clearance details on millions of federal workers, which cybersecurity experts believe could be used in future attacks against the United States.[69] [70]

In the 2014 Quadrennial Defense Review (QDR), the DOD presented its long-range assessment of United States military readiness and plans for the future. By statute, the National Defense Panel (NDP), a nonpartisan ten-member body appointed by Congress, is required to review the QDR's adequacy. The panel concluded that under the Obama administration's military plan "there is a growing gap between the strategic objectives the U.S. military is expected to achieve and the resources required to do so."[71] The significant funding shortfall is "disturbing if not dangerous in light of the fact that global threats and challenges are rising, including a troubling pattern of territorial assertiveness and regional intimidation on China's part, the recent aggression of Russia in Ukraine, nuclear proliferation on the part of North Korea and Iran, a serious insurgency in Iraq that both reflects and fuels the broader sectarian conflicts in the region, the civil war in Syria, and civil strife in the larger Middle East and throughout Africa."[72]

For example, while China expects to have 350 ships by 2020, the NDP report notes that the Obama administration provides for only 260 ships or fewer, which is far less than the 323 to 326 required to meet the potential challenges in the Western Pacific.[73] And despite increasing threats worldwide, the Obama strategy calls for the smallest and oldest air force fleet in modern history, planning a 50 percent reduction to bomber, fighter, and surveillance forces by 2019.[74] The NDP concludes that the Obama defense budget "will increasingly jeopardize our international defense posture and ultimately damage our security, prospects for economic growth, and other interests."[75]

Despite the mounting and diverse national security threats facing the nation, a study conducted by Brookings Institute defense strategist P. W. Singer and his colleagues finds that a majority of younger people consider the United States the world's provocateur. Fifty-seven percent of younger people born between 1980 and 2005 believe America is too involved in global affairs (60 percent of younger Democrats and 50 percent of the group's Republicans share this view).[76] Sixty-six percent of younger people believe that reliance on military force creates hatred toward the United States that, in turn, fosters more terrorism.[77]

The Pew Center for the People and the Press reports a "stark difference across generational lines in how people look back at America's actions prior to the [9/11] attacks. Younger Americans are far more likely to say that there are things the U.S. did wrong in its dealings with other countries that might have motivated the Sept. 11 attacks."[78] In sharp contrast to the governing generation, Pew's polling found that 53 percent of younger people born between 1981 and 2005 believe the United States acted in ways that may have motivated the terrorist attacks.

As the nation has learned time and again, it is American military preparedness and superiority, in combination with a proactive and prudent foreign policy, that are likely to serve as a deterrent to military conflict and prevent large-scale, long-lasting wars. Should war occur—and at times war is unavoidable—the United States must ensure that its young service personnel are the best trained and equipped on the face of the earth. Yet at precisely the time in American history when younger people need to be most vigilant and vocal, given the multiple and rising dangers facing the nation and, sadly, the failure of public officials to adequately prepare for these threats, Pew reports that more than 65 percent of younger people born between 1981 and 2005 support reducing military spending in order to preserve spending on social programs.[79]

Again, it is younger people who are called upon to defend America, American interests, and America's allies against serious and looming national security and military dangers. The DOD "2013 Demographics: Profile of the Military Community" reports that more than one-quarter (25.8 percent) of active duty officers are 41 years of age or older; however, the next-largest age group is 26 to 30 years (22.7 percent), followed by 31 to 35 years (20.4 percent), 36 to 40 years (18.0 percent), and those 25 years or younger (13.2 percent). Even more, nearly one-half (49.4 percent) of active duty enlisted personnel are 25 years of age or younger, with the next-largest age group 26 to 30 years (22.5 percent), followed by 31 to 35 years (13.7 percent), 36 to 40 years (8.8 percent), and those 41 years or older (5.5 percent). Overall, therefore, the average age of the active duty force is 28.6 years. The average age for active duty officers is 34.8 years. And the average age for active duty enlisted personnel is 27.3 years.[80] Should the nation's interests or even survival become so imperiled as to require a draft, it will be younger people who are called upon to take up arms.

On July 17, 1980, in his speech accepting the Republican nomination for president, Ronald Reagan said, in part:

"We are not a warlike people. Quite the opposite. We always seek to live in peace. We resort to force infrequently and with great reluctance—and only after we have determined that it is absolutely necessary. We are awed—and rightly so—by the forces of destruction at loose in the world in this nuclear era. But neither can we be naive or foolish. Four times in my life-time America has gone to war, bleeding the lives of its young men into the sands of beachheads, the fields of Europe, and the jungles and rice paddies of Asia. We know only too well that war comes not when the forces of freedom are strong, but when they are weak. It is then that tyrants are tempted. We simply cannot learn these lessons the hard way again without risking our destruction."[81]

TEN

_____

ON THE CONSTITUTION

WHY SHOULD THE UNITED States Constitution, and the faithful adherence to and execution of it by public officials, matter to younger people? It provides the governing order of a republic intended to protect the individual's liberty from a tyrannical centralized authority and, conversely, the anarchy of mob rule.

On September 17, 1787, at the conclusion of the Constitutional Convention in Philadelphia, delegate James Wilson, on behalf of the ailing Benjamin Franklin, read aloud Franklin's speech to the convention in favor of adopting the Constitution. Franklin stated, in part: "I agree to this Constitution, with all its Faults, if they are such: because I think a General Government necessary for us, and there is no *Form* of

Government but what may be a Blessing to the People if well administered; and I believe farther that this is likely to be well administered for a Course of Years, and can only end in Despotism as other Forms have done before it, when the People shall become so corrupted as to need Despotic Government, being incapable of any other."[1]

Nearly half a century later, Associate Supreme Court Justice Joseph Story, considered one of the great legal thinkers of the nineteenth century, delivered the same warning in August 1834 at the American Institute of Instruction. Among other things, Story explained: "The great mass of human calamities, in all ages, has been the result of bad government, or ill adjusted government; of a capricious exercise of power, a fluctuating public policy, a degrading tyranny, or a desolating ambition."[2] The fundamental objects of all free governments, Story declared, are "the protection and preservation of personal rights, the private property, and the public liberties of the whole people. Without accomplishing these ends, the government may, indeed, be called free, but it is a mere mockery, and a vain, fantastic shadow."[3] Story continued, "Life, liberty, and property stand upon equal grounds in the just estimate of freemen; and one becomes almost worthless without the security of the others. How, then, are these rights to be established and preserved? The answer is, by constitutions of government, wisely framed and vigilantly enforced; by laws and institutions, deliberately examined and steadfastly administered."[4]

Story explained, as Franklin had cautioned, that a constitution, by itself, cannot secure a republic. Nor can reliance on rulers and statesmen alone. The citizenry must be alert and resolute and ensure that those who hold high office uphold the rules of governance. "It is equally indispensable for every American citizen, to enable him to exercise his own rights, to protect his own interests, and to secure the public liberties and just operations of public authority. A republic, by the very constitution of its government, requires, on the part of the people, more vigilance and constant exertion than all others. The American republic, above all others, demands from every citizen unceasing vigilance and exertion; since we have deliberately dispensed with every guard against danger or ruin, except the intelligence and virtue of the people themselves. It is founded on the basis, that the people have wisdom enough to frame their own system of government, and public spirit enough to preserve it; that they cannot be cheated out of their liberties; and that they will not submit to have them taken from them by force. We have silently assumed the fundamental truth, that, as it never can be the interest of the majority of the people to prostrate their own political equality and happiness, so they never can be seduced by flattery or corruption, by the intrigues of faction, or the arts of ambition, to adopt any measures, which shall subvert them. If this confidence in ourselves is justified . . . let us never forget, that it can be justified only by a watchfulness and zeal proportionate to our confidence. Let us never forget, that we must prove ourselves wiser, and better, and purer, than any other nation ever yet has been, if we are to count upon success. Every other republic has fallen by the discords and treachery of its own citizens."[5]

For these purposes and toward these ends, it must first be understood that the Framers established a governmental system that was at once federal, representative, and constitutional. It incorporated the tradition of state sovereignty, upon which the earlier Articles of Confederation had been almost exclusively based, with the necessity of national governance to encourage commerce and trade and guarantee the nation's security and defense. However, and importantly, the authority of the new federal government was to be limited to that which was enumerated, and divided in terms of government responsibilities both within itself and vis-à-vis the several states. Hence, numerous checks and balances were built into and around the federal system.

Moreover, the new federal government was to be a means by which the civil society would be protected and improved, not an end unto itself with the power to bully, control, and ultimately devour the civil society. The primary goal, therefore, was to prevent the centralization of power in the new federal government and to deny a relatively few institutions and public officials the kind of unlimited authority that both corrupts and destroys. Consequently, the Constitution's structure was consistent with the entire rationale behind the American Revolution, as set forth in the Declaration of Independence and infinite speeches and writings during the period. Indeed, it relied in many ways on the thinking of some of the most prominent philosophers of the Enlightenment, especially Charles de Montesquieu, from whom the Framers borrowed their most indispensable idea—*separation of powers*.

As I explained in *Ameritopia*, Montesquieu was a French philosopher who lived from 1689 to 1755. He was the most influential of the French Enlightenment philosophers during the American constitutional period. His seminal work, *The Spirit of the Laws*, had a profound effect on the Framers during the constitutional period. For example, Montesquieu observed that "[t]here are three kinds of government. REPUBLICAN, MONARCHICAL, and DESPOTIC. . . . I assume three definitions, or rather, three facts: one, *republican government is that in which the people as a body, or only a part of the people, have sovereign power; monarchical government is that in which one alone governs, but by fixed and established laws; whereas, in despotic government, one alone, without law and without rule, draws everything along by his will and caprices.*"[6] (Italics in original)

Montesquieu makes the crucial point that unlike other forms of governance, "in a popular [or republican] state there must be an additional spring, which is VIRTUE." "When that virtue ceases, ambition enters those hearts that can admit it, and avarice enters them all. . . . The republic is a cast-off husk, and its strength is no more than the power of a few citizens and the license of all."[7]

Montesquieu was well aware of history's fondness for tyranny, most frequently manifested in the form of concentrated, centralized power in the hands of a few individuals or institutions. He insisted that the best antidote is a fixed, established constitution in which the functions and powers of government are divided among distinct branches. Montesquieu declared: "Political liberty in a citizen is that tranquility of spirit which comes from the opinion each one has of his security, and in order for him to have this liberty the government must be such that one citizen cannot fear another citizen. When legislative power is united with executive power in a single person or in a simple body of magistracy, there is no liberty, because one can fear that the same monarch or senate that makes tyrannical laws will execute them tyrannically. Nor is there liberty if the power of judging is not separate from legislative power and from executive power. If it were joined to legislative power, the power over the life and liberty of the citizens would be arbitrary, for the judge would be the legislator. If it were joined to executive power, the judge could have the force of an op-pressor. All would be lost if the same man or the same body of principal men, either of nobles, or of the people, exercised these three powers: that of making the laws, that of executing public resolutions, and that of judging the crimes or the dis-putes of individuals."[8] These words had a profound influence on the Framers.

In *Federalist 47*, James Madison, in defense of the proposed Constitution and in response to the Antifederalists—who did not believe the lines between and among the three branches of the new federal government were bold enough—insisted that the Framers had been faithful to Montesquieu's maxim on separation of powers. Madison cites Montesquieu by name no fewer than four times in this essay alone, and further underscores that "[t]he oracle who is always consulted and cited on this subject is the celebrated Montesquieu."[9] Madison refuted the naysayers insisting that under the proposed Constitution "[t]he magistrate in whom the whole executive power resides [the president] cannot of himself make a law, though he can put a negative on every law; nor administer justice in person, though he has the appointment of those who do administer it. The judges can exercise no executive prerogative, though they are shoots from the executive stock; nor any legislative function, though they may be advised with by the legislative councils. The entire legislature can perform no judiciary act, though by the joint act of two of its branches the judges may be removed from their offices, and though one of its branches is possessed of the judicial power in the last resort. The entire legislature, again, can exercise no executive prerogative, though one of its branches constitutes the supreme executive magistracy, and another, on the impeachment of a third, can try and condemn all the subordinate officers in the executive department."[10]

The Framers were also heavily influenced by English philosopher John Locke, who lived from 1632 to 1704, and especially by his book *The Second Treatise of Government*. Locke argued, among other things, for the overarching import of elected legislative bodies, for they directly represent the people. Therefore, he insisted, legislatures must not delegate the power of lawmaking to any other entity. Locke wrote: "The legislative cannot transfer the power of making laws to any other hands: for it being but a delegated power from the people, they who have it cannot pass it over to others."[11] Locke continued, "The power of the legislative, being derived from the people by a positive voluntary grant and institutions, can be no other than what the positive grant conveyed, which being only to make laws, and not to make legislators, the legislative can have no power to transfer their authority of making laws and place it in other hands."[12]

The Framers fervently believed they had constructed sufficient divisions of power and distinctive enough roles for each of the federal branches, with certain unavoidable, practicable, but delimited overlapping, providing the citizenry, then and in the future, with a form of republican government consistent with enlightened self-rule. But, again, the people, in the end, would necessarily be required to stand point in the vanguard against would-be overlords and the predictable insatiability of their power lust.

Today, however, the people have not been sufficiently aroused. In fact, despite the overwhelming evidence of the federal government's ubiquity and omnipresence, and its engorgement on all manner of affairs through an ever-expanding and coercive centralized administrative apparatus, too many among the rising generation seem not in the least alarmed by the statists' abandonment of the essential elements of separation of powers.

A healthy civil society and vibrant republic ultimately cannot survive without a properly functioning constitutional system. Consequently, statists relentlessly attack and manipulate the system with endless top-down interventions in human behavior, deceptive and outright false promises tied to government programs and entitlements, and coercive if not oppressive governmental actions, all intended to reshape not only society but the individual. Individual sovereignty—that is, the unalienable individual rights of life, liberty, and the pursuit of happiness—is denounced as a quaint and outdated notion of a bygone era, as are the traditions, customs, and institutions that have developed over time and through generational experience. They must give way to notions of modernity and progressivism, hatched by self-anointed and deluded masterminds who claim to act for "the greater good" and "the public interest," requiring the endless reshuffling and rearranging of society.

In 1848, Karl Marx and Friedrich Engels, writing in *The Communist Manifesto*, declared: "In bourgeois society . . . the past dominates the present; in Communist society, the present dominates the past."[13] This view is shared by contemporary statists, including the current occupants of the White House. On May 14, 2008, the future First Lady of the United States, Michelle Obama, while campaigning for her husband, Barack Obama, proclaimed: "We are going to have to change our conversation; we're going to have to change our traditions, our history. We're going to have to move into a different place as a nation."[14] On October 30, 2008, when the polls showed him the likely winner of the upcoming presidential election, Barack Obama shouted during a campaign stop days before the vote: "We are five days away from fundamentally transforming the United States of America."[15]

Statism and its utopian ends require the subversion of the constitutional order, for the Constitution limits the power of the statists and leaves to the people their own aspirations and pursuits. Unfortunately, as I explained in *Ameritopia*, the nation has already been fundamentally transformed. And as I pointed out in *Liberty and Tyranny*, it is now difficult to describe the nature of the American government. "It is not strictly a constitutional republic, because the Constitution has been and continues to be easily altered by a judicial oligarchy that mostly enforces, if not expands, the Statist's agenda. It is not strictly a representative republic, because so many edicts are produced by a maze of administrative departments that are unknown to the public and detached from its sentiment. It is not strictly a federal republic, because the states that gave the central government life now live at its behest. What, then, is it? It is a society steadily transitioning toward statism."[16]

The product of this degradation, and its effect on a people, is best described by French thinker and philosopher Alexis de Tocqueville. Writing in *Democracy in America*, Tocqueville stated, in part, that this soft tyranny "covers the surface of society with a network of small complicated rules, minute and uniform, through which the most original minds and most energetic characters cannot penetrate, to rise above the crowd. The will of man is not shattered, but softened, bent, and guided; men are seldom forced by it to act, but they are constantly restrained from acting. Such a power does not destroy, but it prevents existence; it does not tyrannize, but it compresses, enervates, extinguishes, and stupefies a people, till each nation is reduced to nothing better than a flock of timid and industrious animals, of which the government is the shepherd."[17] As a result, the virtuousness of the people, essential to the survivability of a republic, is trounced or expunged from the body politic.

The preceding chapters in this book, although necessarily truncated given the practical limits of book writing, bear out Tocqueville's observation. The evidence is unequivocal and overwhelming that much of what the federal government does is without constitutional foundation. In fact, much has been achieved through political and legal deceit and deformation. And, for the most part, the people, particularly younger people, tolerate this, acquiesce to it, if not encourage it.

In *The Liberty Amendments* I noted that "Congress . . . often delegates unconstitutionally lawmaking power to a gigantic yet ever-growing administrative state that, in turn, unleashes on society myriad regulations and rules at such a rapid rate the people cannot possibly know of them . . . and, if by chance, they do, they cannot possibly comprehend them."[18] Moreover, "[h]aving delegated broad lawmaking power to executive branch departments and agencies of its own creation . . . Congress now watches as the president inflates the congressional delegations even further and proclaims repeatedly the authority to rule by executive fiat in defiance of, or over the top of, the same Congress that sanctioned a domineering executive branch in the first place."[19]

The unconstitutional transfer of lawmaking power from Congress to the executive branch and the seizure by the executive branch from Congress of additional lawmaking power have led to disastrous effects.

To demonstrate the problem, consider that each year the executive branch is engaged in frenzied regulatory activity with virtually no oversight by Congress or input from the public. In 2014 alone, the executive branch issued 3,541 regulations,[20] comprising 79,066 pages of the *Federal Register*, the yearly compilation of federal regulations.[21] And these thousands of pages of regulations are piled on top of tens of thousands of pages of regulations from prior years. *Federal Register* page numbers for successive years starting in 2005 are as follows:

|      |        |
|------|--------|
| 2005 | 73,870 |
| 2006 | 74,937 |
| 2007 | 72,090 |
| 2008 | 79,435 |
| 2009 | 68,598 |
| 2010 | 81,405 |
| 2011 | 81,247 |
| 2012 | 78,961 |

| 2013 | 79,311 |
|------|--------|
| 2014 | 79,066 |

That is a total of 768,920 pages of federal regulations in the past ten years.[22]

In addition, the number of actual regulations issued by the executive branch during this period is astounding:

| 2005 | 3,943 |
|------|-------|
| 2006 | 3,718 |
| 2007 | 3,595 |
| 2008 | 3,830 |
| 2009 | 3,503 |
| 2010 | 3,573 |
| 2011 | 3,807 |
| 2012 | 3,708 |
| 2013 | 3,659 |
| 2014 | 3,541 |

That is 36,877[23] regulations, many of which carry heavy fines and penalties, including prison terms upon conviction.

By comparison, Congress, which is supposed to be the federal lawmaking body, has passed the following number of bills in the past ten years:

| 2005 | 161 |
|------|-----|
| 2006 | 321 |

| 2007 | 188 |
| 2008 | 285 |
| 2009 | 125 |
| 2010 | 217 |
| 2011 | 81 |
| 2012 | 127 |
| 2013 | 72 |
| 2014 | 129 |

The purpose here is not to encourage more congressional legislating and meddling in private life, nor to suggest that statistics alone determine the extent of a regulation's reach, as a single overarching regulation can potentially have more economic and societal impact that one hundred regulations. However, these numbers clearly expose the extent to which the basic precept that guides constitutional government has been gutted by both usurpers and abdicators. But this has been the statists' design for more than a century. Indeed, in his 1908 treatise, *Constitutional Government in the United States*, President Woodrow Wilson, a leading advocate for centralized, postconstitutional government, argued that "the President is at liberty, both in law and conscience, to be as big a man as he can. His capacity will set the limit; and if Congress be overborne by him, it will be no fault of the makers of the Constitution,— it will be from no lack of constitutional powers on its part, but only because the President has the nation behind him, and Congress has not."[24] Obviously, Wilson wrote of the Constitution not as it is but as he wanted it to be—stripped of its limits on central power. Wilson's political dogma is on neon display with Barack Obama's conduct as president. Obama has repeatedly defied the limits of his constitutional authority, aggregating powers unto himself in ways past presidents have not. During more than six years as president, Obama has nullified laws, created laws, delayed the implementation of laws, and issued exemptions from and waivers to laws, much of which has been accomplished through executive branch rule making.

For example, despite the fact that Article I, Section I clearly vests legislative power in Congress, the Obama administration has repeatedly altered provisions of the Patient Protection and Affordable Care Act, or Obamacare, including offering employer contributions to members of Congress and their staffs when they purchase insurance on the exchanges created by Obamacare; delaying the deadline for the individual mandate; delaying the deadline for the employer mandate; exempting union reinsurance fees from the law's coverage; creating federal exchanges where states have chosen not to create exchanges; expanding funding of insurer bailouts; and so on.[25]

The Obama administration's Environmental Protection Agency (EPA) has been extremely aggressive in implementing economically crushing regulations, for the most part without congressional authority. It has replaced provisions of the Clean Air Act to claim regulatory control over greenhouse gases and, in turn, vast segments of the American economy.[26] Even Harvard law professor Laurence Tribe found that "[t]he Proposed rule rests on a fatally flawed interpretation of Section 111. According to EPA . . . Congress effectively created two different versions of Section 111, and the agency should be allowed to pick and choose which version it wishes to enforce." "According to EPA, since 1990 the U.S. Code has reflected the wrong version of Section 111, and EPA has discovered a mistake [made by Congress]. According to EPA, both the D.C. Circuit and the U.S. Supreme Court have previously misinterpreted Section 111. According to EPA, the two different versions of Section 111 have created 'ambiguity' triggering deference to the agency's [interpretation]. Every part of this narrative is flawed."[27] Later, Tribe wrote: "[t]he EPA, like every administrative agency, is constitutionally forbidden to exercise powers Congress never delegated to it in the first place. The brute fact is that the Obama administration failed to get climate legislation through Congress. Yet the EPA is acting as though it has the legislative authority anyway to re-engineer the nation's electric generating system and power grid. It does not."[28]

The EPA has done much more. Again without statutory authority, the EPA has also unilaterally replaced provisions of the Clean Water Act to claim regulatory authority over vast areas of land.[29]

In immigration-related matters, Obama has nullified core parts of existing law and substituted for them his own political preferences through unchecked "executive action."[30] After instituting a string of executive directives altering existing im-

migration law, and insisting that if Congress did not act to
adopt his immigration agenda he would act on his own, on
November 20, 2014, just days after the 2014 midterm elections in which the Democratic Party lost the Senate, Obama
took his most far-reaching immigration-related executive
action. Among other things, he ordered the deferral of deportation ("deferred action") of several million illegal aliens,
assigning them temporary legal status, and instituted scores of
additional immigration policy changes. The temporary legal
status results in formerly illegal immigrants receiving extensive taxpayer-subsidized benefits from such programs as Social
Security, Medicare, earned income tax credits, and so on. Robert Rector, senior research fellow at the Heritage Foundation,
estimates the lifetime costs of these benefits to the United
States Treasury at $1.3 trillion.[31]

In a rare judicial rebuke of presidential overreach, and at
the behest of more than two dozen states, U.S. District Judge
Andrew Hanen issued a temporary injunction, writing, in part,
that Obama's executive actions created "a massive change in
immigration practice" affecting "the nation's entire immigration scheme." Moreover, the executive actions did not comply
with the executive branch's own procedures for issuing regulations.[32] There will be more litigation, with the case likely
reaching the U.S. Supreme Court.

Despite Judge Hanen's ruling, for the most part the courts
have upheld executive lawmaking, to the extent they consider
it at all. Even with the judiciary's modern inclination for ac-

tivism and its own penchant for legislating (perhaps because
of them), since the New Deal the courts have essentially given
their imprimatur to the unconstitutional expansion of presidential powers and, conversely, the abridgement of congressional legislating authority, to the great detriment of separation of
powers and, therefore, constitutional government, by rejecting
most challenges to executive branch lawmaking. Meanwhile,
Obama has proclaimed that he will continue to advance his
agenda "by hook or by crook" as he rightly sees few remaining
constitutional impediments to his heavy-handed rule.[33]

Liberty is not an abstraction. It requires private and
public virtue, a just rule of law, and established norms and
institutions—the opposite of fundamental transformation.
The form of government in which these indispensable quali-
ties are best exhibited is a constitutional republic. The pseu-
dointellectual urgency for action to produce the promised
munificence of an idyllic society, while appealing on the surface, exacts a steep price—the disembowelment of the constitutional republic, a result that not so coincidentally serves
the interests of those for whom power is intoxicating, despots
and democrats alike. The rising generation has much to fear
from these circumstances. Yet there is a painful irony, shared
by many younger people, the reasons for which are various
and complicated, in that some view themselves as rebels, of
sorts, challenging authority and "the system" when, in fact,
by their votes and activism, too many habitually contribute
to their own demise and tyranny's rise. Tyranny is not inevi-

table, despite the daunting obstacles to republican restoration; however, if the rising generation does not awaken to challenge these events and stand in its own defense, it will not live in true freedom. It will continue to be exploited under the rule of a progressively coercive and oppressive group of statists for as long as they acquiesce to, if not actively embrace, the design of those who plunder and deceive them. And they will commit future generations to an even more miserable plight.

As his second and last presidential term was winding down, President George Washington thought it fitting to deliver a farewell address to his fellow citizens. The man who was so consequential to the independence and founding of the United States, and the establishment of the American republic, published his final official address on September 19, 1796. He wrote, in part: "It is important . . . that the habits of thinking in a free country should inspire caution in those entrusted with its administration, to confine themselves within their respective constitutional spheres, avoiding in the exercise of the powers of one department to encroach upon another. The spirit of encroachment tends to consolidate the powers of all the departments in one, and thus to create, whatever the form of government, a real despotism. A just estimate of that love of power, and proneness to abuse it, which predominates in the human heart, is sufficient to satisfy us of the truth of this position. The necessity of reciprocal checks in the exercise of political power, by dividing and distributing it into different depositaries, and constituting each the guardian of the public weal against invasions by the others, has been evinced by experiments ancient and modern; some of them in our country and under our own eyes.

"To preserve them must be as necessary as to institute them. If, in the opinion of the people, the distribution or modification of the constitutional powers be in any particular wrong, let it be corrected by an amendment in the way which the Constitution designates. But let there be no change by usurpation; for though this, in one instance, may be the instrument of good, it is the customary weapon by which free governments are destroyed. The precedent must always greatly overbalance in permanent evil any partial or transient benefit, which the use can at any time yield."[34]

_____

# A NEW CIVIL RIGHTS MOVEMENT

AS I ENDED THE previous chapter with President George Washington's Farewell Address of September 19, 1796, I begin this chapter with President Ronald Reagan's Farewell Speech on January 11, 1989. President Reagan encouraged the rising generation to "let 'em know and nail 'em on it"—that is, to push back against teachers, professors, journalists, politicians, and others in the governing generation who manipulate and deceive them:

> An informed patriotism is what we want. And are we doing a good enough job teaching our children what America is and what she represents in the long history of the world? Those of us who are over 35 or so years

of age grew up in a different America. We were taught, very directly, what it means to be an American. And we absorbed, almost in the air, a love of country and an appreciation of its institutions. If you didn't get these things from your family, you got them from the neighborhood, from the father down the street who fought in Korea or the family who lost someone at Anzio. Or you could get a sense of patriotism from school. And if all else failed, you could get a sense of patriotism from the popular culture. The movies celebrated democratic values and implicitly reinforced the idea that America was special. TV was like that, too, through the mid-sixties.

But now, we're about to enter the nineties, and some things have changed. Younger parents aren't sure that an unambivalent appreciation of America is the right thing to teach modern children. And as for those who create the popular culture, well-grounded patriotism is no longer the style. Our spirit is back, but we haven't reinstitutionalized it. We've got to do a better job of getting across that America is freedom—freedom of speech, freedom of religion, freedom of enterprise. And freedom is special and rare. It's fragile; it needs [protection].

So, we've got to teach history based not on what's in fashion but what's important—why the Pilgrims came here, who Jimmy Doolittle was, and what those 30 seconds over Tokyo meant. You know, 4 years ago on the 40th anniversary of D-Day, I read a letter from a young woman writing to her late father, who'd fought on Omaha Beach. Her name was Lisa Zanatta Henn, and she said, "We will always remember, we will never forget what the boys of Normandy did." Well, let's help her keep her word. If we forget what we did, we won't know who we are. I'm warning of an eradication of the American memory that could result, ultimately, in an erosion of the American spirit. Let's start with some basics: more attention to American history and a greater emphasis on civic ritual.

And let me offer lesson number one about America: All great change in America begins at the dinner table. So, tomorrow night in the kitchen, I hope the talking begins. And children, if your parents haven't been teaching you what it means to be an American, let 'em know and nail 'em on it. That would be a very American thing to do.[1]

The consolidation of power, a mortal threat to the individual and liberty, is now the primary object of government. Yet too many are indifferent to the principle of liberty. However, the current societal predicament described in previous chapters, collectively pushing the nation to the brink of catastrophe, is the making not of the rising generation, for it is late to the scene—although it clearly contributes to it—but of the governing generation and its twentieth-century forebears. Somehow the notion that government dispenses freedom and rights, rather than erodes and threatens them when unbounded by constitutional limits, has become an article of faith. Perhaps true liberty is appreciated only by the few. If not, it is time that younger people acquire the knowledge and muster the courage to defend themselves and future generations from big government's reckless and unconscionable designs on the civil society.

This book is, against heavy odds, an appeal to reason and audacity. It is intended for all Americans but particularly the rising generation, which is the primary, albeit not singular, target and casualty of the federal Leviathan's improprieties. It is an appeal to younger people to find the personal strength and will to break through the cycle of statist propaganda and manipulation, unrelenting emotional overtures, and the pressure of groupthink, which are humbling, dispiriting, and absorbing them; to stand up as individuals and collectively against the strong hand of centralized government, which if left unabated will assuredly condemn them to economic and societal calamity.

The challenge is formidable and the outcome uncertain, as is the case with most momentous causes. But there is no alternative short of surrendering to a bleak and miserable fate. There is solace in knowing that throughout history others have stepped forward and successfully led peaceful movements against mighty forces and their injustices. And make no mistake, pillaging America's youth and generations yet unborn is a colossal and disgraceful injustice.

What is required is a New Civil Rights movement—not of the sort that exists today, which has been co-opted by statists, is often led by hucksters, and serves as a surrogate and advocate for centralized government and its pervasive agenda. But a truly new civil rights movement organized around fostering liberty and prosperity for younger people and future generations and against their continued exploitation. Indeed, the well-being of America's younger people through the restoration and then preservation of the nation's founding principles should be the primary objective of public-policy decisions.

For example, the emphasis in education must be on the best interests of the students, not the contractual and bargaining demands of tenured teachers and professors, the virtual monopoly control of education through government schools and public sector unions, the politicization of school curricula for the purpose of indoctrination and social experimentation, and the massive student loan debt young people incur to attend college for a few years, most of which subsidizes out-of-control university spending. This may serve the statists' ends, but it certainly does not improve the education of America's youth.

Immigration policy must no longer focus almost exclusively on the perceived or real interests of the alien, including alien children, while ignoring the economic, cultural, and societal consequences for America's youth and future generations from uninterrupted waves of unassimilated illegal and legal immigration mostly from Third World countries. Ethnic pandering may improve the political lot of statist politicians

looking for electoral advantage, it may serve the interests of
self-appointed leaders of ethnic groups promoting balkanization and demographic advantage, and it may help incom-
petent foreign governments that prefer exporting their next
generation to the United States rather than reforming their
regimes and economic systems, but it certainly is not pursued
in the best interests of America's children and future generations, whose well-being is rarely considered in the making of
these decisions.

Social Security and Medicare were sold to the public as insurance programs. They are not. As such, they now rely mostly
on the "contributions" of younger workers and massive federal
borrowing to subsidize them. Despite repeated and dire warn-
ings about their unsustainable fiscal condition from the trustees appointed to oversee them, younger workers are compelled
to continue to pay into these programs, from which they are
unlikely to benefit upon their retirement and for which future generations will bear the brunt of their eventual collapse.
Even so, the statist resists all relatively painless reforms that
might slow the growth of these programs and enable younger
people to gradually drop out of them. Of course, future generations do not vote in present-day elections. Burdening them
with unimaginable debt has no contemporary political down-
side. These programs are actually worse than a Ponzi scheme,
as the rising generation and its progeny are legally compelled
to serve as a cash cow for as long as they can be milked.

The minimum wage is declared a humane way to increase

the standard of living for low- or unskilled workers. But most individuals who work in these jobs are younger people, many of whom are working in their first jobs, often part-time jobs, learning skills and gaining experience that will help them improve their future employment prospects or start their own small businesses. When the minimum wage is increased, younger people often face layoffs because employers, including franchisees and retailers, are working on thin profit margins or can find less costly alternatives. Moreover, younger people with limited skills who are looking for work are less likely to be hired. Wage increases only matter if, in the first place, you have a job. The statist increases the minimum wage despite its adverse effects on youth employment opportunities.

The politicization and radicalization of the environmental movement into a primitive, degrowth, anticapitalism movement built on a foundation of junk science and emotionalism, and its commandeering of such federal departments as the Environmental Protection Agency and the Interior Department from which it turns countless debilitating and regressive regulations against the private sector, productivity, and innovation, directly threatens two centuries of human progress and the unparalleled American lifestyle. Its campaign to undo the Industrial Revolution and blunt the modern technological revolution will result in economic contraction while further empowering the federal government's grip on daily human activity. The so-called Green Movement is, in fact, an antiliberty and antiopportunity movement aimed at changing the nation in ways that will deprive younger people and future generations of their full potential.

Preserving the peace means being prepared for war. That is history's lesson. The grave and mounting national security threats confronting America today, and the potential for future military conflict, make the simultaneous hollowing out of the United States military and imprudence in the conduct of the nation's foreign policy (particularly in the last decade or so) profoundly challenging to the country generally and the rising generation most predominantly. No group of Americans should be more alert to these gathering storm clouds than younger people, for it is they who fight the wars and, therefore, pay the greatest price.

The national debt—that is, the unfunded liabilities and fiscal operating debt—amounts to *tens of trillions of dollars*. The Government Accountability Office, the Congressional Budget Office, and numerous other public and private institutions have sounded warning alarms about the oncoming crash. But no serious or effective steps have been taken to address this simmering financial and economic implosion. It is, after all, far easier for today's statists to dole out money not yet earned by future generations not yet born and be lauded as compassionate, thereby reaping media plaudits and political benefits for generational wealth redistribution, than to be accused of denying subsidies and programs to a growing list of "worthy" and needy recipients and suffer the media and political backlash. Nonetheless, the governing generation's self-deception (or worse) does not and will not avert the inflating debt bubble, which will eventually burst and flatten the society, turning promises of utopia into the reality of dystopia for future generations.

And at the center of what is left of the American republic is the Constitution. The Constitution is the bedrock on which the nation was built. As Thomas Jefferson explained, "Our peculiar security is in possession of a written Constitution. Let us not make it a blank paper by construction."[2] These days, the law is frequently used by the statists against the individual— to exploit his labor and expropriate his property, to repress his free will and compel his conformity. Rather than securing liberty and ensuring justice through the Constitution's prescriptions and proscriptions, the statists' perversion of law has become the government's most potent weapon against its original purpose. Thwarting the steadily growing tyranny of an illimitable federal government by re-establishing constitutional government is of paramount importance if future generations are to live and prosper in a free and open society.

On October 7, 1771, Samuel Adams declared, "the necessity of the times, more than ever, calls for our utmost circumspection, deliberation, fortitude, and perseverance."[3] Adams's words should echo throughout the land in the form of this New Civil Rights movement of which I speak. It must be a vigorous movement of the rising generation—of younger people who no longer rely almost blindly on the "good intentions" of the statist masterminds and the governing generation who dominate the direction of society, and who have built a governing federal edifice that uses deception and force to plunder their future and, thus, victimize them.

The time has come for the rising generation to turn down the demands and schemes of centralized government, its surrogates, and those who steal from the future and look for ways to influence and drive public policy debates and outcomes in all its forms. It must inject itself into purposes and events that affect its well-being and save the future from those who continually loot it. It must populate the very ranks of the institutions requiring reform to change them from within—such as elective office, the administrative state, teaching positions in public schools and universities, and entertainment and the media. As I explained in *Liberty and Tyranny*: "The Statist does not have a birthright ownership to these institutions. [We] must fight for them, mold them, and where appropriate, eliminate them where they are destructive to the preservation and improvement of the civil society."[4]

This new movement must vigorously and resolutely engage socially, culturally, and politically. From the dinner table, classroom, and workplace, to social clubs, churches, and synagogues; from the backrooms and committee rooms of Congress to the halls of the vast federal bureaucracy; from corporate boardrooms to union halls; from the old media to the new media and social media, the rising generation must make itself known, heard, and felt. It must speak out, challenge, debate, rally, and protest. It must become a force for respectful and prudential activism. And when circumstances are unjust or oppressive, it must even disobey—but in a civil and peaceful way, unlike the violent and destructive rage of the 1960s radical underground movement and its modern adherents.

The rising generation must become the largest and most effective group of activists in the nation for the civil society and America's founding principles, and in so doing help unravel the strangling tentacles of the federal Leviathan and stop the endless march toward a nonexistent utopia and fundamental transformation, through which its demise is assured. It must push America toward restoring its heritage—freedom, prosperity, and republicanism ordered around the Constitution, tradition, and experience—and insist on reformation.[5]

It is the nature of younger people today to passively live and let live and conform to their second-class standing; or worse, if inspired, to unite around distractive or self-destructive causes. But the right cause now is nothing short of self-preservation. And there can be no doubt that the New Civil Rights movement and new generation of activists, which must challenge the tyranny of the status quo, will be met with entrenched resistance, resulting in unease, discomfiture, risk, and ridicule. This is a small price to pay for freedom and justice.

And there is no reason patriotic and enlightened members of the governing generation, including parents and grandparents equally frustrated and alarmed with the future's outlook and equally committed to preserving liberty and prosperity, should not enlist in, if not help drive, this movement—for the benefit of the nation and their offspring. They have much experience, wisdom, and knowledge to contribute to the cause.

The New Civil Rights movement is quintessentially American. Its roots go back to the American Revolution and the country's founding. And Americans have faced and overcome seemingly insuperable challenges in the past, including the Civil War, World War II, and the Cold War. Of course, the New Civil Rights movement is a bloodless struggle; however, in some ways it is more complex. For one, many fellow citizens perceive living and prospering at the expense of others as both a financial entitlement and a right. Furthermore, they see the role of government and the application of law as accomplishing those ends by force if necessary, and the statist is happy to oblige.

Whether knowingly or not, whether by choice or surrender, these citizens have been absorbed into the soft tyranny of an increasingly autocratic government. Although there are fanatics and malcontents among them, the vast majority of these citizens are family members, friends, neighbors, and co-workers.

It is impossible to propose a detailed list of tactical directions or plans pertinent to all settings and valid for all times. Nonetheless, several important suggestions are offered in *Liberty and Tyranny* and *The Liberty Amendments*, the latter of which is an entire dissertation on the subject of the Constitution's Article V Convention of the States process, which empowers the American people, through their state legislatures, to civilly and lawfully reform an oppressive federal gov-

ernment.[6] Armed with the nation's founding principles and
committed to invigorating the civil society, and keenly conscious of the copious evidence of a declining republic and the
disastrous consequences for younger people and future generations, in the spirit and with the vitality of past civil rights
movements, activists and advocates for the New Civil Rights
movement must and, one hopes, will find untold opportunities
and approaches for peaceful and effective recourse. I believe
the greater challenge is, in the first place, awakening younger
people to the cause of their own salvation and the salvation of
future generations so that they may live as free and flourishing
human beings.

Frédéric Bastiat, a brilliant French political and economic
philosopher and deputy to the French Legislative Assembly
who lived from 1801 to 1850, ended his extraordinary book,
*The Law*, with these words:

> God has given to men all that is necessary for them to
> accomplish their destinies. He has provided a social form
> as well as a human form. And these social organs of per-
> sons are so constituted that they will develop themselves
> harmoniously in the clear air of liberty. Away, then, with
> quacks and [government] organizers! Away with their
> rings, chains, hooks and pincers! Away with their arti-
> ficial systems! Away with the whims of governmental
> administrators, their socialized projects, their centraliza-
> tion, their tariffs, their government schools, their state
> religions, their free credit, their bank monopolies, their

regulations, their restrictions, their equalization of taxation, and their pious moralizations! And now that the legislators and do-gooders have so futilely inflicted so many systems upon society, may they finally end where they should have begun: May they reject all systems, and try liberty; for liberty is an acknowledgment of faith in God and His works.[7]

So, I ask the rising generation—America's younger people—what do you choose for yourself and future generations? Do you choose liberty or tyranny? And what do you intend to do about it?

# Acknowledgments

AS IN ALL MY books, I wish to acknowledge how grateful and appreciative I am of my wonderful family. Their encouragement and selflessness gave me the inspiration to spend more than a year of weekends and nights writing this book at the dining room table.

As in the past, thank you to my dear colleagues and friends—Eric Christensen, Richard Hutchison, Michael O'Neill, and Matthew Forys—for their acuity and excellent research assistance; my peerless editor, Mitchell Ivers, who has wisely advised me on five books; and my faithful publisher, Louise Burke, for her enthusiastic support of my book projects. And to my treasured book readers and radio listeners—thank you for your loyalty and patriotism over many years.

Let us all acknowledge that for the reasons set forth in this book, among others, there should be no doubt that we live in perilous times. But for younger people and generations unborn, the challenges are and will be even more formidable, with dire consequences, if the ruling generation does not step up and the rising generation does not wake up. As President Reagan famously declared, "Freedom is never more than one generation away from extinction."[1]

# NOTES

## 1. Plunder and Deceit

1. Francis Bacon, *Of Empire* (New York: Penguin Group, Reprinted from the Essays, edited and introduced by John Pitcher, Penguin Classics, 1985). p. 3.

2. Mark R. Levin, *Liberty and Tyranny* (New York: Simon & Schuster, 2009), pp. 3–4.

3. Edmund Burke, *Reflections on the Revolution in France* (London: Seeley, 1872), p. 93.

4. Edmund Burke, appearing in *James Fenimore Cooper: New Historical and Literary Contexts*, W. M. Verhoeven, ed. (Atlanta: Cooper, 1993), p. 56.

5. Charles de Montesquieu, *The Spirit of the Laws*, Anne M. Cohler, Basia C. Miller, and Harold S. Stone, eds. (Cambridge, U.K.: Cambridge University Press, 2009), Part 1, Book 3, Chapter 3.

6. Patrick O'Connor, "Poll Finds Widespread Economic Anxiety," *Wall Street Journal*, August 6, 2014, A4.

7. James Madison, *The Federalist No. 51* (New York: Signet Classics, 2003), p. 319.

8. Mark R. Levin, *Ameritopia* (New York: Simon & Schuster, 2013), p. 7.

9. Alexis de Tocqueville, *Democracy in America*, vol. 2 (New York: Knopf Everyman's Edition, 1994), p. 319.

10. Pew Research Center, "Millennials in Adulthood," March 7, 2014, http://www.pewsocialtrends.org/2014/03/07/millennials-in-adulthood/.

11. Mark R. Levin, *Liberty and Tyranny* (New York: Simon & Schuster, 2009), pp. 9–10.

12. Eric Hoffer, *The True Believer* (New York: Harper & Row, 1951), p. 69.

13. Bruce Thornton, "Is Leftist School Indoctrination Unstoppable?" *Frontpage Magazine*, February 27, 2013, http://www.frontpagemag.com/2013/bruce-thornton/is-leftist-school-indoctrination-unstoppable/print/.

14. Karl Marx, *The Communist Manifesto* (London: Soho, 2010), p. 19.

15. Id.

16. Pew Research Center, "Millennials in Adulthood," March 7, 2014, http://www.pewsocialtrends.org/2014/03/07/millennials-in-adulthood/.

17. Federal Reserve Bank of New York, "Student Loan Debt by Age Group," March 29, 2013, http://www.newyorkfed.org/studentloandebt/.

18. Bureau of Labor Statistics, "Employment status of the civilian population by sex and age," March 6, 2015, http://www.bls.gov/news.release/empsit.t01.htm.

19. Jaison R. Abel and Richard Deitz, "Are the Job Prospects of Recent College Graduates Improving?" Liberty Street Economics,

September 4, 2014, http://libertystreeteconomics.newyorkfed.org/2014/09/are-the-job-prospects-of-recent-college-graduates-improving.html#.VRWervm3SlK.

20. Pew Research Center, "The Rising Cost of Not Going to College," February 11, 2014, http://www.pewsocialtrends.org/2014/02/11/the-rising-cost-of-not-going-to-college/.

21. Pew Research Center, "In Post-Recession Era, Young Adults Drive Continuing Rise in Multi-Generational Living," July 17, 2014, http://www.pewsocialtrends.org/2014/07/17/in-post-recession-era-young-adults-drive-continuing-rise-in-multi-generational-living/.

22. Congressional Budget Office, "The 2014 Long-Term Budget Outlook," July, 2014, https://www.cbo.gov/sites/default/files/45471-Long-TermBudgetOutlook_7-29.pdf.

23. "Thomas Jefferson to John Wayles Eppes, 11 September 1813," Founders Online, National Archives, http://founders.archives.gov/documents/Jefferson/03-06-02-0388 (last update: 2015-03-20). Source: *The Papers of Thomas Jefferson, Retirement Series*, vol. 6, 11 March to 27 November 1813, J. Jefferson Looney, ed. (Princeton, N.J.: Princeton University Press, 2009), pp. 490–99.

24. "Thomas Jefferson to Samuel Kercheval, 12 July 1816," Online Library of Liberty, http://oll.libertyfund.org/titles/808. Source: *The Works of Thomas Jefferson*, vol. XII, Paul Leicester Ford, ed. (New York and London: G.P. Putnam's Sons, 1904–5).

## 2. On the Debt

1. Walter Williams, "A Minority View: Spending and Morality," George Mason University, July 9, 2014, http://econfaculty.gmu.edu/wew/articles/14/SpendingAndMorality.htm.

2. Walter Williams, "A Minority View: Spending and Morality," George Mason University, July 9, 2014, http://econfaculty.gmu.edu/wew/articles/14/SpendingAndMorality.htm.

3. Thomas Sowell, "A Taxing Experience: Cut the National Debt By Reducing Spending," *Capitalism Magazine*, November 25, 2004, http://capitalismmagazine.com/2004/11/a-taxing-experience-cut-the-national-debt-by-reducing-spending/.

4. "The Debt to the Penny and Who Holds It," Treasury Direct, http://www.treasurydirect.gov/NP/debt/current.

5. Calculated using the U.S. Census Bureau's estimate of U.S. population as of July 1, 2014. Table 1. Annual Estimates of the Resident Population for the United States, Regions, States, and Puerto Rico: April 1, 2010, to July 1, 2014, available at http://www.census.gov/popest/data/national/totals/2014/index.html.

6. Kimberly Amadeo, "U.S. Debt by President: By Dollar and Percent: Why the Winner is . . . Barack Obama," January 26, 2015, http://useconomy.about.com/od/usdebtanddeficit/p/US-Debt-by-President.htm (last visited April 12, 2015).

7. Christopher J. Conover, " 'Not One Dime': Health Care Law Projected to Add $6.2 Trillion to U.S. Deficit," American Enterprise Institute, March 14, 2013, http://www.aei.org/publication/not-one-dime-health-care-law-projected-to-add-6-2-trillion-to-u-s-deficit/; Brian M. Riedl, "Why Government Spending Does Not Stimulate Economic Growth: Answering the Critics," The Heritage Foundation Backgrounder #2354, January 5, 2010, http://www.heritage.org/research/reports/2010/01/why-government-spending-does-not-stimulate-economic-growth-answering-the-critics.

8. C. Eugene Steuerle, "Paying a Price for Decisions of Yesteryear,"

Urban Institute, August 12, 2007, http://www.urban.org/retire
ment_policy/url.cfm?ID=901106.

9. "The 2014 Long-Term Budget Outlook," Congressional Budget Office, July 2014, p. 1, https://www.cbo.gov/sites/default
/files/45471-Long-TermBudgetOutlook_7-29.pdf.

10. Id.

11. "Table 1.1—SUMMARY OF RECEIPTS, OUTLAYS, AND
SURPLUSES OR DEFICITS (–): 1789–2019," Office of Man-
agement and Budget, http://www.whitehouse.gov/omb/budget
/Historicals.

12. Id.

13. "List of Large Caps," www.onlineinvestor.com/large_caps (last
visited January 3, 2015).

14. Id., pp. 8–9.

15. Id., p. 1.

16. Id.

17. Id.

18. Kasia Klimasinska and Jeanna Smialck, "Obama's Sweet Spot
May Sour as Deficit Seen Wider in 2016," Bloomberg, October 14, 2014, http://www.bloomberg.com/news/2014-10-14
/obama-s-sweet-spot-may-sour-as-deficit-seen-wider-in-2016
.html.

19. CBO Report, p. 14.

20. Peter Morici, "Misguided Government Policies Are Stifling
Economic Growth," Money News, April 3, 2014, http://www
.moneynews.com/Peter-Morici/growth-labor-jobs-economic
/2014/04/03/id/563432/.

21. "Table 1.2—SUMMARY OF RECEIPTS, OUTLAYS, AND
SURPLUSES OR DEFICITS (–) AS PERCENTAGES OF

GDP: 1930–2019," Office of Management and Budget, http://www.whitehouse.gov/omb/budget/Historicals.

22. Id.

23. Id.

24. Id.

25. "The 2014 Long-Term Budget Outlook," Congressional Budget Office, July 2014, p. 3, https://www.cbo.gov/sites/default/files/45471-Long-TermBudgetOutlook_7-29.pdf.

26. Id., p. 6.

27. Id., p. 3.

28. Id., p. 15.

29. James D. Agresti, "National Debt Facts," April 26, 2011, updated December 3, 2014, www. Justfacts.com/nationaldebt.asp#quantifying (last visited January 3, 2015) (chart calculated using Table 3.16: "Government Current Expenditures by Function." U.S. Department of Commerce, Bureau of Economic Analysis, http://www.bea.gov/iTable/iTable.cfm, and Report: "Fiscal Year 2014 Historical Tables: Budget of the U.S. Government," White House Office of Management and Budget, http://www.whitehouse.gov/sites/default/files/omb/budget/fy2014/hist.pdf.

30. Id.

31. "A Summary of the 2014 Annual Reports," Social Security Administration, July 2014, http://www.ssa.gov/oact/trsum/.

32. "The 2014 Long-Term Budget Outlook," Congressional Budget Office, July 2014, p. 47, https://www.cbo.gov/sites/default/files/45471-Long-TermBudgetOutlook_7-29.pdf.

33. Id.

34. Id., p. 20.

35. Id.

36. Id.

37. Id., p. 42.

38. Id.

39. Id., p. 44.

40. Charles S. Clark, "Comptroller warns government debt is unsustainable." Government Executive, February 12, 2013, http://www.govexec.com/oversight/2013/02/comptroller-warns -government-debt-unsustainable/61260/.

41. Id.

42. GAO-14-319R—Financial Audit, General Accounting Office, February 27, 2014, p. 1.

43. Laurence J. Kotlikoff, "America's Fiscal Insolvency and Its Generational Consequences," Testimony to the Senate Budget Committee, February 25, 2015, http://www.budget.senate .gov/republican/public/index.cfm?a=Files.Serve&File_id=5e 791473-386f-4149-8db0-00e50fdcdbf8, p. 2.

44. Id., pp. 3–4.

45. Id., p. 5.

46. Id., p. 6.

47. Id., p. 9.

48. Meg Handley, "How the National Debt Affects You," U.S. News & World Report, March 31, 2011, www.money.usnews.com /money/personal-finance/articles/2011/03/31/how-the-national -debt-affects-you; J. D. Foster, "The Many Real Dangers of Soaring National Debt," Heritage Foundation, Backgrounder #2814, June 18, 2013, www.heritage.org/research/reports/2013/06/the -many-real-dangers-of-soaring-national-debt.

49. "The 2014 Long-Term Budget Outlook," Congressional Budget Office, July 2014, p. 13, https://www.cbo.gov/sites/default /files/45471-Long-TermBudgetOutlook_7-29.pdf.

50. Id.

51. Id.

52. Id., pp. 13–14.

53. "Why is Fiscal Responsibility Important?" The Concord Coalition, www.concordcoalition.org/print/issues/primers/why-fiscal -resonsibility-important (quoting Edward M. Gramlich, Federal Reserve Board governor, June 2004).

54. Id.

55. Laurence J. Kotlikoff, "America's Fiscal Insolvency and Its Generational Consequences," Testimony to the Senate Budget Committee, February 25, 2015, http://www.budget.senate.gov /republican/public/index.cfm?a=Files.Serve&File_id=5e791473 -386f-4149-8db0-00e50fdcdbf8, p. 9.

56. Josh Zumbrun, "Younger Generation Faces a Savings Deficit," *Wall Street Journal*, November 9, 2014, http://www.wsj.com/ar ticles/savings-turn-negative-for-younger-generation-1415572405.

57. Id.

58. "Ultimate Guide to Retirement," CNN Money, http://money .cnn.com/retirement/guide/basics_basics.moneymag/index7.htm (last visited January 5, 2015).

59. Josh Zumbrun, "Younger Generation Faces a Savings Deficit," *Wall Street Journal*, November 9, 2014, http://www.wsj .com/articles/savings-turn-negative-for-younger-generation-1415 572405.

60. Blake Ellis, "40 million Americans now have student loan debt," CNN Money, September 10, 2014, http://money.cnn .com/2014/09/10/pf/college/student-loans/.

61. Id.

62. Id.

63. Diana ElBoghdady, "Student debt may hurt housing recovery

by hampering first time buyers," *Washington Post*, February 17, 2014, http://www.washingtonpost.com/business/economy/student-debt-may-hurt-housing-recovery-by-hampering-first-time-buyers/2014/02/17/d90c7c1e-94bf-11e3-83b9-1f024193bb84_story.html.

64. Gary R. Maltola, "The Financial Capability of Young Adults—A Generational View," FINRA Investor Education Foundation, March 2014, p. 7.

65. Id.

66. Bonnie McGeer, "Millennial Morass: Worrisome Trends for a Debt-Ridden Generation," *American Banker*, November 21, 2013, http://www.americanbanker.com/magazine/123_12/millennial-morass-worrisome-trends-for-a-debt-ridden-generation-1063604-1.html.

67. Id.

68. Id.

69. Hadley Malcolm, "Millennials' ball-and-chain: Student loan debt," *USA Today*, July 1, 2013, http://www.usatoday.com/story/money/personalfinance/2013/06/30/student-loan-debt-economic-effects/2388189/.

70. Id.

71. Bruce Drake, "6 new findings about Millennials," Pew Research Center, March 2, 2014, http://www.pewresearch.org/fact-tank/2014/03/07/6-new-findings-about-millennials/.

72. Press Release, "New Census Bureau Statistics Show How Young Adults Today Compare With Previous Generations In Neighborhoods Nationwide," U.S. Census Bureau, December 4, 2014, http://www.census.gov/newsroom/press-releases/2014/cb14-219.html.

73. Id.

74. Bureau of Economic Analysis, "Gross Domestic Product: Fourth Quarter and Annual 2014 (Third Estimate)." March 27, 2015, http://www.bea.gov/newsreleases/national/gdp/2015/pdf /gdp4q14_3rd.pdf.

75. Laura Saunders, "Top 20% of Earners Pay 84% of Income Tax," *Wall Street Journal*, April 11, 2015, B8.

76. George Washington, "Farewell Address, 1796," The Avalon Project, Yale Law School, http://avalon.law.yale.edu/18th_cen tury/washing.asp.

**3. On Social Security**

1. Social Security Administration, "Research Note #19: Social Security Benefits as a Percentage of Total Federal Budget Expenditures," http://www.ssa.gov/history/percent.html; Center on Budget and Policy Priorities, "Policy Basics: Where Do Our Federal Tax Dollars Go?" March 31, 2014, http://www.cbpp.org /cms/?fa=view&id=1258.

2. Social Security Administration (SSA), Monthly Statistical Snapshot, May 2014, Table 2, http://www.socialsecurity.gov/ policy/docs/quickfacts/stat_snapshot/index.html, Social Security Administration, Social Security Beneficiary Statistics, "Number of beneficiaries receiving benefits on December 31, 1970–2013," http://www.socialsecurity.gov/OACT/STATS/OASDIbenies .html.

3. Social Security Administration, History, "Ratio of Social Security Covered Workers to Beneficiaries Calendar Years 1940–2010," http://ssa.gov/history/ratios.html. The ratio in 2013 was 2.8. Social Security Administration, 2014 OASDI Trustees Report, "Covered Workers and Beneficiaries, Calendar Years 1945–2090,"

Table IV.B.2, http://www.ssa.gov/oact/tr/2014/IV_B_LRest.html #493869.

4. Social Security Administration, 2014 OASDI Trustees Report, "Covered Workers and Beneficiaries, Calendar Years 1945–2090," Table IV.B.2, http://www.ssa.gov/oact/tr/2014/IV_B_LRest.html #493869.

5. As of December 31, 2013, according to the administration's chief actuary, there were 57,978,610 total recipients. Social Security Administration, Social Security Beneficiary Statistics, "Number of beneficiaries receiving benefits on December 31, 1970–2013," http://www.socialsecurity.gov/OACT/STATS/OA SDIbenies.html.

6. Social Security Administration, "Understanding the Benefits 2014," p. 5, http://www.ssa.gov/pubs/EN-05-10024.pdf. Note that the self-employed pay Self Employment Contributions Act (SECA) taxes and not FICA taxes.

7. Social Security Administration, "Social Security & Medicare Tax Rates," http://www.ssa.gov/oact/ProgData/taxRates.html.

8. Social Security Administration, "Contribution and Benefits Base," http://www.ssa.gov/oact/cola/cbb.html.

9. Dawn Nuschler, Congressional Research Service, "Social Security Primer," June 17, 2013, p. 4.

10. Associated Press, "New Retirees Receiving Less in Social Security Than They Paid in, Marking Historic Shift," August 2, 2012, http://www.foxnews.com/politics/2012/08/07/new-retirees -receiving-less-in-social-security-than-paid-in-marking-historic/.

11. Laurence Kotlikoff, "44 Social Security 'Secrets' All Baby Boomers and Millions of Current Recipients Need to Know— Revised!" *Forbes*, July 3, 2012, http://www.forbes.com/sites

/kotlikoff/2012/07/03/44-social-security-secrets-all-baby-boomers -and-millions-of-current-recipients-need-to-know/.

12. Associated Press, "New Retirees Receiving Less in Social Security Than They Paid in, Marking Historic Shift," August 2, 2012, http://www.foxnews.com/politics/2012/08/07/new-retirees -receiving-less-in-social-security-than-paid-in-marking-historic/.

13. Social Security Administration, A Summary of the 2014 Annual Reports, http://www.ssa.gov/oact/trsum/.

14. Id. Note that this is the same year predicted in the previous Annual Report.

15. Id.

16. The 2014 Annual Report of the Board of Trustees of the Federal Old-Age and Survivors Insurance and Federal Disability Insurance Trust Funds, p. 191, http://www.ssa.gov/oact/tr/2014 /tr2014.pdf; A Summary of the 2013 Annual Reports, Table IV.B6.—Unfunded OASDI Obligations Through the Infinite Horizon, Based on Intermediate Assumptions, http://www.ssa .gov/oact/tr/2013/IV_B_LRest.html#417122.

17. Henry Hazlitt, *Economics in One Lesson* (New York: Three Rivers Press, 1979), pp. 16–17.

18. Id., p. 16.

19. Milton Friedman, "Social Security Socialism," *Wall Street Journal*, January 26, 1999, A18.

20. Larry DeWitt, Social Security Administration, "Research Note #23 Luther Gulick Memorandum re: Famous FDR Quote," July 21, 2005, http://www.ssa.gov/history/Gulick.html.

21. Mark R. Levin, *Liberty and Tyranny: A Conservative Manifesto* (New York: Threshold Editions, 2009), p. 98.

22. Robert J. Myers and Richard L. Vernaci, *Within the System:*

My *Half Century in Social Security* (Winsted, Conn.: ACTEX Publications, 1992), pp. 93–94, as quoted in Gary Sidor, Congressional Research Service, "Fact Sheet: The Social Security Retirement Age," January 24, 2013, p. 1.

23. Franklin Roosevelt's Statement on Signing the Social Security Act, August 14, 1935, http://docs.fdrlibrary.marist.edu/odssast .html (emphasis added).

24. Eric Pianin, "CBO Warns Unchecked Entitlement Spending Is 'Unsustainable,'" *Fiscal Times*, July 16, 2014, http://www.thefiscal times.com/Articles/2014/07/16/CBO-Warns-Unchecked-Enti tlement-Spending-Unsustainable#sthash.PoH0feEm.L72B8J4M .dpuf.

25. Social Security Administration, "The 2014 OASDI Trustees Report." Letter to the Hon. John Boehner, July 28, 2014, http:// ssa.gov/oact/TR/2014/709letter_DI_House_2014.pdf (emphasis added).

26. Rep. Raul Grijalva, Letter to President Obama, October 15, 2010, http://big.assets.huffingtonpost.com/Letter3.pdf; Dave Johnson, "Over 100 Members of Congress Demand Deficit Commission Keep Hands Off Social Security," Campaign for America's Future Blog, November 15, 2010, http://ourfuture.org/20101115 /Over_100_Members_Of_Congress_Demand_Deficit_Commis sion_Keep_Hands_Off_Social_Security.

27. Michael D. Tanner, "Piketty Gets It Wrong." Cato Institute Blog, April 23, 2014, http://www.cato.org/publications/commentary /piketty-gets-it-wrong.

28. Herbert Stein, "Herb Stein's Unfamiliar Quotations." Slate, May 15, 1997, http://www.slate.com/articles/business/it_seems_to _me/1997/05/herb_steins_unfamiliar_quotations.single.html.

## 4. On Medicare and Obamacare

1. Centers for Medicare and Medicaid Services, "NHE Fact Sheet," http://www.cms.gov/Research-Statistics-Data-and-Sys tems/Statistics-Trends-and-Reports/NationalHealthExpend Data/NHE-Fact-Sheet.html.

2. Dan Munro, "Annual U.S. Healthcare Spending Hits $3.8 Trillion," *Forbes*, February 2, 2014, http://www.forbes.com/sites /danmunro/2014/02/02/annual-u-s-healthcare-spending-hits -3-8-trillion/.

3. The World Bank, "Health expenditure, total (% of GDP)," http://data.worldbank.org/indicator/SH.XPD.TOTL.ZS.

4. Patricia A. Davis, "Medicare: Part B Premiums." Congressional Research Service, March 12, 2014, p. 1, https://www.fas.org/sgp /crs/misc/R40082.pdf.

5. Penny Starr, "11,588,500 Words: Obamacare Regs 30x as Long as Law," CNSNews.com, October 14, 2013, http://cnsnews.com /news/article/penny-starr/11588500-words-obamacare-regs-30x -long-law.

6. Social Security Administration, "A SUMMARY OF THE 2014 ANNUAL REPORTS," http://www.ssa.gov/oact/trsum/.

7. "The 2014 Long-Term Budget Outlook," Congressional Budget Office, July 2014, p. 3, https://www.cbo.gov/sites/default/files /45471-Long-TermBudgetOutlook_7-29.pdf.

8. National Association of State Budget Officers, "State Expenditure Report (Fiscal 2012–2014 Data)," p. 49, http://www.nasbo .org/sites/default/files/State%20Expenditure%20Report%20 %28Fiscal%202012-2014%29S.pdf.

9. Kimberly Leonard, "Americans Vote Against Greater Medicaid Reach," *U.S. News & World Report*, November 5, 2014, http://

www.usnews.com/news/articles/2014/11/05/us-voters-say-no-to
-obamacare-medicaid-expansion.

10. Jason Millman, "Obamacare paradox: Medicaid is expanding, but doctors are facing a huge pay cut," *Washington Post*, Wonkblog, December 10, 2014, http://www.washingtonpost.com/blogs/wonkblog/wp/2014/12/10/obamacare-paradox-medicaid-is-expanding-but-doctors-are-facing-a-huge-pay-cut/.

11. Nina Owcharenko, "Why the Obamacare Medicaid Expansion Is Bad for Taxpayers and Patients," The Heritage Foundation, March 5, 2013, http://www.heritage.org/research/reports/2013/03/why-the-obamacare-medicaid-expansion-is-bad-for-taxpayers-and-patients.

12. http://www.foxnews.com/politics/2015/06/07/medicaid-expansion-under-obamacare-raising-costs-concerns-for-opt-in-states/.

13. "The 2014 Long-Term Budget Outlook," Congressional Budget Office, July 2014, p. 3, https://www.cbo.gov/sites/default/files/45471-Long-TermBudgetOutlook_7-29.pdf.

14. Id., pp. 3–4.

15. Social Security Administration, Social Security History, "Remarks with President Truman at the Signing in Independence of the Medicare Bill," http://www.ssa.gov/history/lbjstmts.html.

16. Id.

17. Patricia A. Davis, "Medicare: Part B Premiums," Congressional Research Service, March 12, 2014, Summary, https://www.fas.org/sgp/crs/misc/R40082.pdf.

18. C. Eugene Steuerle and Richard B. Fisher, "How Lifetime Benefits and Contributions Point the Way Toward Reforming Our Senior Entitlement Programs," National Institute for Health Care Management Foundation, August 2011, http://nihcm.org

/images/stories/EV-Steuerle-Rennane-FINAL.pdf, and C. Eugene Steuerle and Stephanie Rennane, "Social Security and Medicare Taxes and Benefits Over a Lifetime," Urban Institute, June 2011, http://www.urban.org/UploadedPDF/social-security-medicare -benefits-over-lifetime.pdf.

19. Social Security Administration, A Summary of the 2014 Annual Reports, http://www.ssa.gov/oact/trsum/.

20. Centers for Medicare and Medicaid Services, 2014 Annual Report of the Boards of Trustees of the Federal Hospital Insurance and Federal Supplemental Medical Insurance Trust Funds, p. 9.

21. Id., p. 70.

22. American Medical Association, "Overview of the RBRVS," http://www.ama-assn.org/ama/pub/physician-resources/solutions -managing-your-practice/coding-billing-insurance/medicare/the -resource-based-relative-value-scale/overview-of-rbrvs.page.

23. Peter Whoriskey and Dan Keating, "How A Secretive Panel Uses Data That Distorts Doctors' Pay," *Washington Post*, http:// www.washingtonpost.com/business/economy/how-a-secretive -panel-uses-data-that-distorts-doctors-pay/2013/07/20/ee134e3a -eda8-11e2-9008-61e94a7ea20d_story.html.

24. Kathleen M. King, Testimony Before the Subcommittee on Oversight and Investigations, Committee on Energy and Commerce, House of Representatives, "Medicare Fraud: Further Actions Needed to Address Waste, Fraud and Abuse," June 25, 2014, http://www.gao.gov/assets/670/664381.pdf.

25. Id.

26. American Medical Association, "CPT® Process—How a Code Becomes a Code," http://www.ama-assn.org/ama/pub /physician-resources/solutions-managing-your-practice/coding -billing-insurance/cpt/cpt-process-faq/code-becomes-cpt.page.

27. Julie Miller, Behavioral Healthcare, "What you need to know about the latest ICD-10 rule, August 1, 2014, http://www.behavioral.net/article/what-you-need-know-about-latest-icd-10-rule.

28. Anna Wilde Mathews, "Walked into a Lamppost? Hurt While Crocheting? Help Is on the Way," *Wall Street Journal*, September 13, 2011, http://online.wsj.com/news/articles/SB10001424053111904103404576560742746021106?mg=reno64-wsj&url=http%3A%2F%2Fonline.wsj.com%2Farticle%2FSB10001424053111904103404576560742746021106.html.

29. Id.

30. Department of Health and Human Services, Office of Inspector General, "Improper Payments for Evaluation and Management Services Cost Medicare Billions in 2010," May 2014, p. 16, http://oig.hhs.gov/oei/reports/oei-04-10-00181.pdf.

31. Id.; Charles Ornstein, "Medicare Overpays Billions for Office Visits, Patient Evaluations," Pro Publica, May 28, 2014, http://www.propublica.org/article/medicare-overpays-billions-for-office-visits-patient-evaluations.

32. Romina Boccia, Alison Acosta Fraser, and Emily Goff, "Federal Spending by the Numbers, 2013: Governmental Spending Trends in Graphics, Tables, and Key Points," Heritage Foundation, August 20, 2013, http://www.heritage.org/research/reports/2013/08/federal-spending-by-the-numbers-2013.

33. 42 U.S.C. § 10891.

34. 42 U.S.C. § 18022; Healthcare.gov, "Essential Health Benefits," https://www.healthcare.gov/glossary/essential-health-benefits/.

35. Scott Gottlieb, "Health Plan Premiums Are Skyrocketing According to New Survey of 148 Insurance Brokers, with Delaware Up 100%, California 53%, Florida 37%, Pennsylvania 28%," *Forbes*, April 7, 2014, http://www.forbes.com/sites/scott

gottlieb/2014/04/07/health-plan-premiums-are-skyrocketing
-according-to-new-survey-of-148-insurance-brokers-analysts
-blame-obamacare/.

36. Amy Finkelstein, "The Cost of Coverage," *Wall Street Journal*,
February 28, 2007, http://economistsview.typepad.com/econo
mistsview/2007/02/amy_finkelstein.html.

37. "What We're Learning: Reducing Inappropriate Emergency
Department Use Requires Coordination with Primary Care,"
Robert Wood Johnson Foundation, September 2013, http://www
.rwjf.org/content/dam/farm/reports/issue_briefs/2013/rwjf407773.

38. Laura Ungar, "More patients flocking to ERs under Obamacare,"
(Louisville, Ky.) *Courier-Journal*, June 8, 2014, http://www
.usatoday.com/story/news/nation/2014/06/08/more-patients
-flocking-to-ers-under-obamacare/10173015/.

39. Merritt Hawkins, "2014 Survey: Physician Appointment Wait
Times and Medicaid and Medicare Acceptance Rates," p. 6,
http://www.merritthawkins.com/uploadedFiles/MerrittHawkins
/Surveys/mha2014waitsurvPDF.pdf.

40. Id.

41. Kelli Kennedy, "Obamacare Impacts Primary Care Doctor
Shortage," Associated Press, December 7, 2014.

42. Sarah Kliff, "Romney's right: Obamacare cuts Medicare by $716
billion. Here's how," *Washington Post*, August 14, 2012, http://www
.washingtonpost.com/blogs/wonkblog/wp/2012/08/14/romneys
-right-obamacare-cuts-medicare-by-716-billion-heres-how/.

43. David Leonhardt, "After the Great Recession," *New York Times*,
May 3, 2009, MM36.

44. 42 U.S.C. § 1395kkk.

45. F. A. Hayek, *The Road to Serfdom: Text and Documents—The*

*Definitive Edition* (The Collected Works of F. A. Hayek, Vol. 2), Bruce Caldwell, ed. (New York: Routledge, 2014), p. 114.

## 5. On Education

1. Mark Dixon, *U.S. Census Bureau, Public Education Finances: 2012*, G12-CG-ASPEF, U.S. Govt. Printing Office, Washington, D.C., p. 11, http://www2.census.gov/govs/school/12f33pub.pdf.

2. "How much money does the United States spend on public elementary and secondary schools?" Fast Facts, National Center for Education Statistics, U.S. Department of Education, http:// nces.ed.gov/fastfacts/display.asp?id=66.

3. Mark Dixon, *U.S. Census Bureau, Public Education Finances: 2012*, G12-CG-ASPEF, U.S. Govt. Printing Office, Washington, D.C., http://www2.census.gov/govs/school/12f33pub.pdf.

4. Kathryn M. Doherty, Sandi Jacobs, and Martin F. Lueken, *Doing the Math on Teacher Pensions*, National Council on Teacher Quality, January 2015, http://nctq.org/dmsView/Doing_the_Math.

5. The Digest of Education Statistics: 2012, National Center for Education Statistics, U.S. Department of Education, http:// nces.ed.gov/programs/digest/d13/tables/dt13_605.10.asp.

6. Program for International Student Assessment, December 2013, "Selected Findings from PISA 2012," http://nces.ed.gov/surveys /pisa/pisa2012/index.asp.

7. Id.

8. The term "education systems" is used here to differentiate individual systems within nations, as well as national systems.

9. Program for International Student Assessment, December 2013, "Selected Findings from PISA 2012," http://nces.ed.gov/surveys /pisa/pisa2012/index.asp.

10. "2013 SAT Report on College and Career Readiness," September 26, 2013, The College Board, http://media.collegeboard.com/homeOrg/content/pdf/sat-report-college-career-readiness-2013.pdf.

11. Lindsey Burke, "Our National Report Card: No Education Progress Since 2009," National Review Online, May 13, 2014, http://www.nationalreview.com/corner/377899/our-national-report-card-no-education-progress-2009-lindsey-burke.

12. 2013 Mathematics and Reading: Grade 12 Assessments, National Assessment of Educational Progress ("NAEP"), "Are the nation's twelfth-graders making progress in mathematics and reading?" http://www.nationsreportcard.gov/reading_math_g12_2013/#/.

13. Council on Foreign Relations, Joel I. Klein and Condoleezza Rice, Task Force Chairs, U.S. Education Reform and National Security, Independent Task Force Report No. 68, 2012, p. 9, http://www.cfr.org/united-states/us-education-reform-national-security/p27618.

14. Andrew J. Coulson, "State Education Trends Academic Performance and Spending Over the Past 40 Years," Policy Analysis, Cato Institute, March 18, 2014, http://object.cato.org/sites/cato.org/files/pubs/pdf/pa746.pdf.

15. Id.

16. Mike Antonucci, "The Long Reach of Teachers Unions, Education Next," Fall 2010, http://educationnext.org/files/ednext_20104_24.pdf.

17. "Firing tenured teachers: Our view," USA Today, June 16, 2014, http://www.usatoday.com/story/opinion/2014/06/16/teacher-tenure-los-angeles-vergara-editorials-debates/10640909/.

18. The Pew Forum on Education Reform, "A Tribute to Al Shanker," August 1993, http://big.assets.huffingtonpost.com

/shankerpew_0.pdf. Marcus Baram, "Is Teachers Union Scrubbing Al Shanker's Legacy?" Huffington Post, October 14, 2010, http://www.huffingtonpost.com/2010/10/14/is-teachers-union-scrubbi_n_763029.html.

19. *Vergara* v. *California*, No. BC484642 (Cal. Sup. Ct. L.A., tentative decision filed June 10, 2014), http://studentsmatter.org/wp-content/uploads/2014/06/Tenative-Decision.pdf.

20. Id., p. 8.

21. Id., p. 13.

22. Scholastic Lesson Plan, "Multiculturalism and Diversity," http://www.scholastic.com/teachers/lesson-plan/multiculturalism-and-diversity. Allie Bidwell, "Obama Wants Kids to Learn About Global Warming," *U.S. News & World Report*, December 3, 2014, http://www.usnews.com/news/articles/2014/12/03/obama-administration-to-launch-global-warming-education-initiative. Adam B. Lerner, "AP U.S. History controversy becomes a debate on America," Politico, February 21, 2015, http://www.politico.com/story/2015/02/ap-us-history-controversy-becomes-a-debate-on-america-115381.html.

23. Claire Suddath, "Tossing the First Lady's Lunch," *Bloomberg Business*, August 21, 2014, http://www.bloomberg.com/bw/articles/2014-08-21/school-districts-avoid-nutrition-rules-by-shunning-federal-funds.

24. "Fast Facts," U.S. Department of Education, National Center for Education Statistics, 2013, Digest of Education Statistics, Chapter 3, http://nces.ed.gov/fastfacts/display.asp?id=76.

25. Federal Reserve Bank of New York, Quarterly Report on Household Debt and Credit, November 2014, http://www.newyorkfed.org/householdcredit/2014-q3/data/pdf/HHDC_2014Q3.pdf.

26. Ecreditdaily, "Student Loan Delinquencies Worse Than Previ-

ously Known; One-Third Late on Payments," March 28, 2015, http://ecreditdaily.com/2015/03/student-loan-delinquencies -worse-than-previously-known-one-third-late-on-payments/.

27. Richard Fry, Kim Parker, and Molly Rohal, *Young Adults, Student Debt and Economic Well-being*, Pew Research Center's Social and Demographic Trends Project, 2014, p. 4.

28. Id., p. 5.

29. Josh Zumbrun, "It Only Takes $10,400 to Be Richer Than Most Millennials," *Wall Street Journal*, September 4, 2014, http:// blogs.wsj.com/economics/2014/09/04/it-only-takes-10400-to -be-richer-than-most-millennials/; Board of Governors of the Federal Reserve System, "2013 Survey of Consumer Finances," October 20, 2014, http://www.federalreserve.gov/econresdata/scf /scfindex.htm.

30. "Top 20 Richest Colleges for 2013: The Biggest Endowments," April 21, 2014, ThinkAdvisor.com, http://www.thinkadvisor .com/2013/04/02/top-10-richest-colleges-for-2012the-biggest -endowm?page_all=1.

31. "U.S. Spotlight on Statistics: Back to College," p. 7, "College and University Employment Increasing," September 2010, http://data.bls.gov/cgi-bin/print.pl/spotlight/2010/college/home .htm.

32. Id., p. 8.

33. Id., p. 9.

34. "Employer Costs for Employee Compensation—March 2014," News Release, June 11, 2014, Bureau of Labor Statistics, U.S. Department of Labor, http://www.bls.gov/news.release/pdf/ecec .pdf.

35. Andrew Martin, "Building a Showcase Campus, Using an I.O.U.," *New York Times*, December 13, 2012, http://www.ny

times.com/2012/12/14/business/colleges-debt-falls-on-students
-after-construction-binges.html?pagewanted=all&_r=0.

36. Id.

37. Id.

38. Id.

39. Michael Grunwald, "The College Loan Bombshell Hidden in
the Budget," Politico, February 5, 2015, http://www.politico.com
/magazine/story/2015/02/the-college-loan-bombshell-hidden
-in-the-budget-114930.html#.VOyFMPm3SlI.

40. Id.

41. Id.

42. Scott Jaschik, "Moving Further to the Left," *Inside Higher
Education*, October 24, 2012, https://www.insidehighered.com
/news/2012/10/24/survey-finds-professors-already-liberal-have
-moved-further-left.

43. Id.

44. Dalton Conley, *You May Ask Yourself: An Introduction to Thinking
Like a Sociologist* (New York: W.W. Norton & Company, 2013).

45. Daniel B. Klein and Charlotta Stern, *Groupthink in Academia:
Majoritarian Departmental Politics and the Professional Pyramid*,
*Independent Review*, Spring 2009, p. 594.

46. Id.

47. http://www.foxnews.com/us/2015/05/13/liberal-speakers-dominate
-college-commencements-says-conservative-group/.

48. Allan Bloom, *The Closing of the American Mind: How Higher
Education Has Failed Democracy and Impoverished the Souls of
Today's Students* (New York: Simon & Schuster, 1987), p. 380.

49. Id., p. 382.

## 6. On Immigration

1. Samuel P. Huntington, *Who Are We? The Challenges to America's National Identity* (New York: Simon & Schuster, 2005), p. 195.

2. U.S. Census Bureau, "Statistic Abstract of the United States, Section 31, 20th Century Statistics, Immigration, by Leading Country or Region of Last Resident: 1901 to 1997," http://www.census.gov/prod/99pubs/99statab/sec31.pdf.

3. Id.

4. The Honorable Jeff Sessions, "Immigration Handbook for the New Republican Majority," January 2015, http://www.sessions.senate.gov/public/_cache/files/67ae7163-6616-4023-a5c4-534c53e6fc26/immigration-primer-for-the-114th-congress.pdf; Steve Camarota and Karen Zeigler, "All Employment Growth Since 2000 Went to Immigrants," Center for Immigration Studies, June 2014, http://cis.org/sites/cis.org/files/camarota-employment_0.pdf (data derived and analyzed from U.S. Census Bureau data collected from 2009 to 2011).

5. Jie Zong and Jeanne Batalova, "Frequently Requested Statistics on Immigrants and Immigration in the United States," Migration Policy Institute, February 26, 2015, http://www.migrationpolicy.org/article/frequently-requested-statistics-immigrants-and-immigration-united-states#Current and Historical.

6. Theodore H. White, *America in Search of Itself: The Making of the President 1956–1980* (New York: Warner, 1982).

7. Mark R. Levin, *Liberty and Tyranny* (New York: Simon & Schuster, 2009), p. 151.

8. The Honorable Jeff Sessions, "Immigration Handbook for The New Republican Majority," January 2015, http://www.sessions.senate.gov/public/_cache/files/67ae7163-6616-4023-a5c4-534c53e6fc26/immigration-primer-for-the-114th-congress.pdf.

9. Editorial, "President Obama's unilateral action on immigration has no precedent," *Washington Post*, December 3, 2014, http://www.washingtonpost.com/opinions/president-obamas-unilateral-action-on-immigration-has-no-precedent/2014/12/03/3fd7865 0-79a3-11e4-9a27-6fdbc612bff8_story.html.

10. Samuel P. Huntington, *Who Are We? The Challenges to America's National Identity* (New York: Simon & Schuster, 2005), p. 180.

11. Id., p. 184.

12. Id., p. 185.

13. Id., p. 196.

14. Steve Camarota, "Immigrants in the United States, 2010: A Profile of America's Foreign-Born Population," Center for Immigration Studies, August 2012, http://www.cis.org/sites/cis.org/files/articles/2012/immigrants-in-the-united-states-2012.pdf.

15. Id.

16. Congressional Budget Office, "The Economic Impact of S. 744, the Border Security, Economic Opportunity, and Immigration Modernization Act," June 2013, http://www.cbo.gov/sites/default/files/cbofiles/attachments/44346-Immigration.pdf.

17. U.S. Chamber of Commerce, "Why Our Current Immigration System Does Not Work for the Business Community," http://immigration.uschamber.com/reforms/why-our-current-immigration-system-does-not-work-for-the-business-community.

18. National Restaurant Association, "Ask the operator," http://www.restaurant.org/News-Research/News/Ask-the-Operator.

19. Benjamin W. Powell and Art Carden, "Why Is Immigration Illegal Anyway?" Independent Institute, November 20, 2011, http://www.independent.org.

20. Id.

21. Id.

22. Steve Camarota and Karen Zeigler, "Are There Really Jobs Americans Won't Do?" Center for Immigration Studies, May 2013, http://cis.org/are-there-really-jobs-americans-wont-do (data derived and analyzed from U.S. Census Bureau data collected from 2009 to 2011).

23. Id.

24. Id.

25. (Author name redacted), "Presentation of Data on the U.S. Foreign Born, Average Incomes of the Bottom 90% of Tax Filers, and the Estimated Share of Income Held by the Bottom 90% of the U.S. Income Distribution, 1945–2013." Congressional Research Service, April 22, 2015, http://www.scribd.com/doc/262874867/CRS-Income-and-Foreign-Born-Population.

26. Hal Salzman, Daniel Kuehn, and B. Lindsay Lowell, "Guestworkers in the High-Skill U.S. Labor Market." EPI Briefing Paper # 359, April 24, 2013, Economic Policy Institute, http://s3.epi.org/files/2013/bp359-guestworkers-high-skill-labor-market-analysis.pdf.

27. Id.

28. Id.

29. Byron York, "Business pushes immigration reform even as it lays off American workers," *Washington Examiner*, October 3, 2013, http://www.washingtonexaminer.com/business-pushes-immigration-reform-even-as-it-lays-off-american-workers/article/2536800. The Honorable Jeff Sessions, *Immigration Handbook for the New Republican Majority*, January 15, 2015, http://www.sessions.senate.gov/public/_cache/files/67ae7163-6616-4023-a5c4-534c53e6fc26/immigration-primer-for-the-114th-congress.pdf.

30. U.S. Census Bureau, "Census Bureau Reports Majority of STEM

College Graduates Do Not Work In STEM Occupations," Release Number CB14-130, July 10, 2014, http://www.census .gov/newsroom/press-releases/2014/cb14-130.html.

31. Hal Salzman, Daniel Kuehn, and B. Lindsay Lowell, "Guest-workers in the High-Skill U.S. Labor Market," EPI Briefing Paper # 359, April 24, 2013, Economic Policy Institute, http:// s3.epi.org/files/2013/bp359-guestworkers-high-skill-labor-market -analysis.pdf.

32. Id.

33. Id.

34. Id.

35. Bureau of Labor Statistics, "Labor force status of 2013 high school graduates and 2012–2013 high school dropouts 16 to 24 years old by school enrollment, educational attainment, sex, race, and Hispanic or Latino ethnicity, October 2013," http:// data.bls.gov/cgi-bin/print.pl/news.release/hsgec.t01.htm.

36. Eric Ruark, "Generation Jobless—The Unemployment Crisis of Millennials," Federation for American Immigration Reform, February 2014, http://www.fairus.org/DocServer/research-pub /Generation-Jobless_Feb2014_rev.pdf.

37. Id.

38. Id.

39. Andrew Sum and Ishwar Khatiwada, "Still Young, Restless, and Jobless: The Growing Employment Malaise Among U.S. Teens and Young Adults," Center for Labor Market Studies, Northeastern University, January 2004, http://www.aypf.org /publications/stillyoungrestlessandjoblessreport.pdf.

40. Id.

41. Id.

42. Id.

43. Id.

44. Id.

45. Id.

46. Richard Fry, "A Rising Share of Young Adults Live in Their Parents' Home," Pew Research Social & Demographical Trends, August 1, 2013, http://www.pewsocialtrends.org/2013/08/01/a -rising-share-of-young-adults-live-in-their-parents-home/.

47. Id.

48. Id.

49. Id.

50. Steven Camarota and Karen Zeigler, "All Employment Growth Since 2000 Went to Immigrants," Center for Immigration Studies, June 2014, http://cis.org/all-employment-growth-since -2000-went-to-immigrants (data derived and analyzed from Current Population Survey for the first quarters of 2000 and 2014).

51. Id.

52. Bureau of Labor Statistics, "Labor Force Statistics from the Current Population Survey," http://data.bls.gov/pdq/SurveyOut putServlet.

53. Eric Ruark, "Generation Jobless—The Unemployment Crisis of Millennials," Federation for American Immigration Reform, February 2014, http://www.fairus.org/DocServer/research-pub /Generation-Jobless_Feb2014_rev.pdf.

54. Bureau of Labor Statistics, "Civilian labor force participation rates by age, sex, race, and ethnicity," December 2013, http:// data.bls.gov/cgi-bin/print.pl/emp/ep_table_303.htm.

55. Id.

56. Id.

57. Richard Fry, "A Rising Share of Young Adults Live in Their

Parents' Home," Pew Research Social & Demographic Trends, August 1, 2013, http://www.pewsocialtrends.org/2013/08/01/a-rising-share-of-young-adults-live-in-their-parents-home/.

58. Milton Friedman, "Illegal Immigration, Part 1," Lecture, https://www.youtube.com/watch?v=3eyJIbSgdSE.

59. Samuel P. Huntington, *Who Are We? The Challenges to America's National Identity* (New York: Simon & Schuster, 2005), p. 219.

60. Robert Rector and Jason Richwine, Ph.D., "The Fiscal Cost of Unlawful Immigrants and Amnesty to the U.S. Taxpayer," Heritage Foundation, May 6, 2013, http://thf_media.s3.amazonaws.com/2013/pdf/sr133.pdf.

61. Id.

62. Congressional Budget Office, "How Changes in Immigration Policy Might Affect the Federal Budget," January 2015, http://www.cbo.gov/sites/default/files/cbofiles/attachments/49868-Immigration.pdf.

63. Id.

64. Paul Lewis, "Congressman warns of 'civil war' among Democrats unless Obama acts on Immigration," *Guardian*, November 3, 2014, http://www.theguardian.com/us-news/2014/nov/03/luis-gutierrez-obama-civil-war-deportation-immigration. Eric Kayne, "Census: White majority in U.S. gone by 2043," NBC News, June 13, 2013, http://usnews.nbcnews.com/_news/2013/06/13/18934111-census-white-majority-in-us-gone-by-2043.

65. J. Christian Adams, "Homeland Security Working Overtime to Add 'New Americans' by 2016 Election," PJMedia.com, April 23, 2015, http://pjmedia.com/jchristianadams/2015/04/23/homeland-security-working-overtime-to-add-new-americans-by-2016-election/#ixzz3YEbnp9EV.

66. Steven A Camarota and Karen Zeigler, "Immigrant Population to Hit Highest Percentage Ever in 8 Years," Center for Immigration Studies, April 2015, http://cis.org/sites/cis.org/files/immigration-population-highest_0.pdf.

67. Pew Research Center, "American Values Survey," April 2015, http://www.people-press.org/values-questions/q40n/more-restrictions-on-people-coming-to-live-in-our-country/#race.

68. Lydia Saad, "More in U.S. Would Decrease Immigration than Increase," Gallup, June 27, 2014, http://www.gallup.com/poll/171962/decrease-immigration-increase.aspx.

69. Alistair Bell, "Americans worry that illegal migrants threaten way of life, economy," Reuters, August 7, 2014, http://www.reuters.com/article/2014/08/07/us-usa-immigration-worries-id USKBN0G70BE20140807.

**7. On the Environment**

1. "Ex-EPA official told lawmakers of project to 'modify the DNA' of capitalism," January 22, 2014, Fox News, http://www.foxnews.com/politics/2014/01/22/ex-epa-official-told-lawmakers-project-to-modify-dna-capitalism/print. John Beale, "Deposition of John C. Beale," Committee on Oversight and Government Reform, U.S. House of Representatives, December 19, 2013, http://oversight.house.gov/wp-content/uploads/2014/01/Beale-Deposition.pdf.

2. Naomi Klein, "Naomi Klein says climate activists need to get comfortable attacking capitalism," Grist.org, October 9, 2014, http://grist.org/climate-energy/naomi-klein-says-climate-activists-need-to-get-comfortable-attacking-capitalism/.

3. Barack Obama, interview with *San Francisco Chronicle* edito-

rial board, January 17, 2008, https://www.youtube.com/watch?v=HlTxGHn4sH4.

4. Barack Obama, interview with *San Francisco Chronicle* editorial board, January 17, 2008, https://www.youtube.com/watch?v=DpTIhyMa-Nw.

5. Degrowth.org, "Definition," http://www.degrowth.org/definition-2.

6. Clubfordegrowth.org, "Our Philosophy," http://clubfordegrowth.org/our_philosophy/.

7. Federico Demaria, Fraccios Schneider, Filka Sekulaova, and Joan Martinez-Alier, *What Is Degrowth? From Activist Slogan to a Social Movement, Environmental Values* 22 (2013): 191–215, White Horse Press.

8. Id.

9. Id.

10. Id.

11. Id.

12. Serge Latouche, "The globe downshifted," *Le Monde diplomatique*—English edition, January 13, 2006, http://mondediplo.com/2006/01/13degrowth.

13. Id.

14. Social PreCOP Preparatory Meeting, "Margarita Declaration on Climate Change," July 15–18, 2014, http://www.precopsocial.org/sites/default/files/archivos/margarita_declaration_on_climate_change.pdf.

15. Federico Demaria, Fraccios Schneider, Filka Sekulaova, and Joan Martinez-Alier, *What Is Degrowth? From Activist Slogan to a Social Movement, Environmental Values* 22 (2013): 191–215, White Horse Press.

16. Id.

17. Mackenzie Mount, "Green Biz: Work Less to Live More," www .sierraclub.org.

18 Serge Latouche, "The globe downshifted," *Le Monde diplomatique*—English edition, January 13, 2006, http://monde diplo.com/2006/01/13degrowth.

19. Id.

20. Karl Marx and Friedrich Engels, *The Communist Manifest* (London: Soho, 2010), p. 21.

21. Ayn Rand (Peter Schwartz, ed.), *Return of the Primitive—The Anti-Industrial Revolution* (Meridian [Penguin], 1999), pp. 281, 282.

22. Id., p. 285.

23. Id., p. 286.

24. Id.

25. Mark J. Perry, "18 spectacularly wrong apocalyptic predictions made around the time of the first Earth Day in 1970, expect more this year," American Enterprise Institute, April 21, 2014, http:// www.aei.org/publication/18-spectacularly-wrong-apocalyptic -predictions-made-around-the-time-of-the-first-earth-day-in -1970-expect-more-this-year/print/.

26. John Brignell, "A Complete List of Things Caused by Global Warming," Numberwatch, July 16, 2008, http://www.number watch.co.uk/warmlist.htm; Mark R. Levin, *Liberty and Tyranny* (New York: Simon & Schuster, 2009), pp. 140–43.

27. Executive Order No. 12,291, 46 Fed. Reg. 13,193 (1981).

28. Regulatory Development and Retrospective Review Tracker, Archived Rulemakings, http://yosemite.epa.gov/opei/RuleGate .nsf/content/archivedrules.html?opendocument.  Regulatory

Development and Retrospective Review Tracker, Rulemakings by Phase: Final Rule Published, http://yosemite.epa.gov/opei /RuleGate.nsf/content/phasesfinal.html?opendocument.

29. Id.

30. James E. McCarthy and Claudia Copeland, "EPA Regulations: Too Much, Too Little, or On Track?" Congressional Research Service, July 8, 2014, https://fas.org/sgp/crs/misc/R41561.pdf.

31. Regulatory Development and Retrospective Review Tracker, Rules by Projected Publication Date, http://yosemite.epa.gov /opei/RuleGate.nsf/content/upcoming.html?opendocument.

32. Id.

33. Nicolas Loris and Filip Jolevski, "EPA's Climate Regulations Will Harm American Manufacturing," Heritage Foundation, Issue Brief, March 4, 2014, http://thf_media.s3.amazonaws.com /2014/pdf/IB4158.pdf.

34. Gregory Clark, *A Farewell to Alms, A Brief Economic History of the World* (Princeton, N.J.: Princeton University Press, 2007), p. 1.

35. Id.

36. Robert Rector and Rachel Sheffield, "Understanding Poverty in the United States: Surprising Facts About America's Poor," The Heritage Foundation, September 13, 2011, http://thf_media .s3.amazonaws.com/2011/pdf/bg2607.pdf.

37. Id.

38. Kenneth Pomeranz, *The Great Divergence: China, Europe and the Making of the Modern World Economy* (Princeton, N.J.: Princeton University Press, 2000), p. 61. Also see Gregory Clark, *A Farewell to Alms, A Brief Economic History of the World* (Princeton, N.J.: Princeton University Press, 2007), p. 260.

39. Gregory Clark, *A Farewell to Alms, A Brief Economic History of the World* (Princeton, N.J.: Princeton University Press, 2007), p. 260.

40. Kenneth Pomeranz, *The Great Divergence: China, Europe and the Making of the Modern World Economy* (Princeton, N.J.: Princeton University Press, 2000), p. 283.

41. Id., pp. 283–84.

42. Gregory Clark, *A Farewell to Alms, A Brief Economic History of the World* (Princeton, N.J.: Princeton University Press, 2007), p. 260.

43. Id.

44. Id., p. 272.

45. Id., p. 260.

46. Id., p. 277.

47. Mark R. Levin, *Liberty and Tyranny* (New York: Simon & Schuster, 2009), pp. 125–26.

48. Nicolas Loris, "Man's Contribution to Global Warming" *Daily Signal*, March 27, 2009, http://dailysignal.com/2009/03/27/man%E2%80%99s-contribution-to-global-warming/.

49. *Statement of Patrick Moore, Ph.D., Before the Senate Environment and Public Works Committee, Subcommittee on Oversight,* February 25, 2014, http://www.epw.senate.gov/public/index.cfm?FuseAction=Files.View&FileStore_id=415b9cde-e664-4628-8fb5-ae3951197d03.

50. Diane Bast, "30,000 Scientists Sign Petition on Global Warming," Heartlander.org, July 1, 2008, http://news.heartland.org/print/23387.

51. *Massachusetts v. Environmental Protection Agency*, 549 U.S. 497 (2007).

52. *Standards of Performance for Greenhouse Gas Emissions for New*

*Stationary Sources: Electric Utility Generating Units*, 79 Federal Register 1430.

53. Eileen O'Grady, "Southern Co. delays advanced coal plant to 2015 amid rising costs," April 29, 2014, www.Reuters.com.

54. *Carbon Pollution Emission Guidelines for Existing Stationary Sources: Electric Generating Units*, 79 Fed. Reg. 34,830.

55. Parker Gallant, "Ontario's Power Trip: Irrational energy planning has tripled power rates under the Liberals' direction," *Financial Post*, June 2, 2014, www.financialpost.com.

56. Id.

57. The White House, Office of the Press Secretary. "Administration Takes Steps Forward on Climate Action Plan by Announcing Actions to Cut Methane Emissions," January 14, 2015, http://www.whitehouse.gov/the-press-office/2015/01/14/fact-sheet-administration-takes-steps-forward-climate-action-plan-anno-1; Coral Davenport, "Obama Is Planning New Rules on Oil and Gas Industry's Methane Emissions," *New York Times*, January 13, 2015, http://www.nytimes.com/2015/01/14/us/politics/obama-administration-to-unveil-plans-to-cut-methane-emissions.html?_r=0.

58. http://www2.epa.gov/sites/production/files/2015-06/documents/hf_es_erd_jun2015.pdf.

59. TransitionNetwork.org, "Energy Descent Action Plans," https://www.transitionnetwork.org/.

60. TransitionNetwork.org, "Policies for Transition," https://www.transitionnetwork.org/.

61. *Federal Water Pollution Control Act* (the "Clean Water Act") 33 U.S.C. §§ 1251–1387.

62. 33 U.S.C. § 1251(b).

63. *Definition of "Waters of the United States" Under the Clean Water Act*, 79 Fed. Reg. 22,188.

64. Ayn Rand (Peter Schwartz, ed.), *Return of the Primitive—The Anti-Industrial Revolution* (Meridian [Penguin], 1999), pp. 288, 289.

## 8. On the Minimum Wage

1. "Employment Situation Summary," Economic News Release, Bureau of Labor Statistics, April 3, 2015, http://www.bls.gov /news.release/empsit.nr0.htm.

2. Id.

3. Labor Force Statistics from the Current Population Survey, "Charting the Labor Market: Data from the Current Population Survey," Bureau of Labor Statistics, April 3, 2015, http://www .bls.gov/web/empsit/cps_charts.pdf.

4. "Survey of the Unemployed Shows 47% Say They Have 'Completely Given Up' Looking for a Job," Express Employment Professionals (Harris Poll), May 21, 2014, http://www.express pros.com.

5. "Employment Situation Summary," Economic News Release, Bureau of Labor Statistics, April 3, 2015, http://www.bls.gov /news.release/empsit.nr0.htm.

6. Labor Force Statistics from the Current Population Survey, "Charting the Labor Market: Data from the Current Population Survey," Bureau of Labor Statistics, April 3, 2015, http://www .bls.gov/web/empsit/cps_charts.pdf.

7. "How the Government Measures Unemployment," Bureau of Labor Statistics, http://www.bls.gov.

8. United States Senate, Committee on the Budget, "Nearly 1 in 4 Americans in Prime Working Years Are Not Employed," http:// www.budget.senate.gov/republican/public/index.cfm/charts.

9. "Employment Situation Summary," Economic News Release,

Bureau of Labor Statistics, April 3, 2015, http://www.bls.gov/news.release/empsit.nr0.htm.

10. Id.

11. Mary Lorenz, "Millennials vs. Baby Boomers: Who 'Won' the Recession?" June 9, 2014, http://thehiringsite.careerbuilder.com/2014/06/09/millennials-vs-baby-boomers-won-recession/.

12. Id.

13. "Employment Situation Summary," Economic News Release, Bureau of Labor Statistics, April 3, 2015, http://www.bls.gov/news.release/empsit.nr0.htm.

14. Id.

15. President Barack Obama, "Remarks by the President on Signing of Executive Order," February 12, 2014, http://www.whitehouse.gov.

16. President Barack Obama, "Obama slams GOP over minimum wage vote," CNN Political Ticker (posted by Jim Acosta), April 30, 2014, http://politicalticker.blogs.cnn.com.

17. President Barack Obama, "Remarks by the President on Signing of Executive Order," February 12, 2014, http://www.whitehouse.gov.

18. American Legislative Exchange Council, "Raising the Minimum Wage: The Effects on Employment, Businesses and Consumers," ALEC.org, March, 2014, http://www.alec.org/wp-content/uploads/Raising_Minimum_wage.pdf.

19. Id.

20. David Neumark and William L. Wascher, *Minimum Wages* (Cambridge, Mass.: MIT Press, 2008), p. 12.

21. Id.

22. Id., p. 14.

23. *Adkins v. Children's Hospital*, 261 U.S. 525, 554-556 (1923).

24. David Neumark and William L. Wascher, *Minimum Wages* (Cambridge, Mass.: MIT Press, 2008), p. 15.

25. *West Coast Hotel Co.* v. *Parrish*, 300 U.S. 379.

26. U.S. Department of Labor, *Federal Minimum Wage Rates Under the Fair Labor Standards Act*, http://www.dol.gov.

27. Mark Wilson, *The Negative Effects of Minimum Wage Laws*, Policy Analysis, Cato Institute, June 21, 2012, www.cato.org.

28. Harold L. Cole and Lee E. Ohanian, *New Deal Policies and the Persistence of the Great Depression: A General Equilibrium Analysis*, research memo, Department of Economics, UCLA, February 2003.

29. Id.

30. U.S. Department of Labor, *Federal Minimum Wage Rates Under the Fair Labor Standards Act*, http://www.dol.gov.

31. "Characteristics of Minimum Wage Workers," BLS Reports, 2013, U.S. Bureau of Labor Statistics Report 1048, March 2014, www.bls.gov.

32. Id.

33. Id.

34. Id.

35. President Barack Obama, "Remarks by the President on Signing of Executive Order," February 12, 2014, http://www.whitehouse.gov.

36. Id.

37. David Neumark and William L. Wascher, *Minimum Wages* (Cambridge, Mass.: MIT Press, 2008), p. 39.

38. Id.

39. Id., p. 51.

40. Mark Wilson, *The Negative Effects of Minimum Wage Laws*, Policy Analysis, Cato Institute, June 21, 2012, www.cato.org.

41. Assunta Ng, "Blog: What SeaTac tells us about $15 minimum wage," *Asian Weekly*, May 22, 2014, http://wwwnwasianweekly .com.

42. David Neumark and William L. Wascher, *Minimum Wages* (Cambridge, Mass.: MIT Press, 2008), p. 289.

43. Id., p. 287.

44. Id., p. 291.

45. Id., p. 290.

46. Id., p. 291.

47. Congressional Budget Office, "The Effects of a Minimum-Wage Increase on Employment and Family Income," February 2014, http://www.cbo.org.

48. Id.

**9. On National Security**

1. "National Security Strategy of the United States," White House, January 1987, p. 6, nssarchive.us/NSSR/1987.pdf.

2. Id.

3. "National Security Strategy of the United States," White House, August 1991, p. 1, http://nssarchive.us/NSSR/1991.pdf.

4. Judah Grunstein, "Russia Annexes Georgian Provinces on the Installment Plan," *World Politics Review*, October 29, 2008, http://www.worldpoliticsreview.com/trend-lines/2838/russia -annexes-georgian-provinces-on-the-installment-plan.

5. Thomas Frear, Łukasz Kulesa, and Ian Kearns, "Dangerous Brinkmanship: Close Military Encounters Between Russia and the West in 2014," European Leadership Network, November 2014, p. 1, http://www.europeanleadershipnetwork.org/media library/2014/11/09/6375e3da/Dangerous%20Brinkmanship.pdf.

6. Damien Sharkov, "'Biggest NATO Reinforcement Since Cold

War' Sets Frontlines Against Russia," *Newsweek*, February 5, 2015, http://www.newsweek.com/biggest-nato-reinforcement -cold-war-sets-frontlines-russian-threat-304722.

7. Frear, Kulesa, and Kearns, p. 1.

8. Id.

9. Richard Javad Heydarian, "America's Next Big Challenge: Countering China's Diplomatic Blitzkrieg," *The National Interest*, November 30, 2014, http://nationalinterest.org/feature /americas-next-big-challenge-countering-china%E2%80%99s -diplomatic-11754?page=2.

10. Javier Blas, "China still trumps the competition in Africa Inc.," *Financial Times*, October 9, 2014, http://www.ft.com /cms/s/0/87075f26-4eda-11e4-b205-00144feab7de.html#axzz3 OorlYpVg; Simon Romero and Alexei Barrionuevo, "Deals Help China Expand Sway in Latin America," *New York Times*, April 15, 2009, http://www.nytimes.com/2009/04/16/world /16chinaloan.html?_r=0.

11. Max Fisher, "Why China still supports North Korea, in six little words," *New York Times*, February 12, 2013, http://www .washingtonpost.com/blogs/worldviews/wp/2013/02/12/why -china-still-supports-north-korea-in-six-little-words/.

12. Michael Peel, "Iran, Russia and China prop up Assad economy," *Financial Times*, June 27, 2013, http://www.ft.com/intl /cms/s/0/79eca81c-df48-11e2-a9f4-00144feab7de.html#axz z3OorlYpVg.

13. Merv Mogollon and Chris Kraul, "Venezuela's president hits road to save ailing economy," *LA Times*, January 5, 2015, http://www .latimes.com/world/mexico-americas/la-fg-venezuela-president -economy-20150105-story.html.

14. Eli Lake, "Iran's nuclear program helped by China, Russia," *Washington Times*, July 5, 2011, http://www.washingtontimes .com/news/2011/jul/5/irans-nuclear-program-helped-by-china -russia/?page=all.

15. http://www.wsj.com/articles/chinas-island-building-poses -dilemma-for-u-s-1433102116.

16. Tara Murphy, "Security Challenges in the 21st Century Global Commons," *Yale Journal of International Affairs*, Spring/Summer 2010, pp. 28, 34.

17. Id.

18. Kris Osborn, "China's Fleet Advancing Faster Than U.S. Expected," *Defense Tech*, February 5, 2014, http://defensetech.org /2014/10/29/chinas-submarine-fleet-takes-historic-steps-forward/.

19. Jesse L. Karotkin, "Trends in China's Naval Modernization," Office of Naval Intelligence, Testimony before the U.S.-China Economic and Security Review Commission, January 30, 2014, http://news.usni.org/2014/02/03/document-chinas-naval-mod ernization.

20. Id.

21. Murphy, p. 35.

22. Id.

23. Tony Capaccio, "Iran Speaks More Softly But Keeps Building Bigger Sticks," *Bloomberg*, August 20, 2014, http://www.bloom berg.com/news/2014-08-20/iran-speaks-more-softly-but-keeps -building-bigger-sticks.html.

24. Murphy, p. 35.

25. Capaccio, op. cit.

26. James R. Clapper, "Worldwide Threat Assessment of the U.S. Intelligence Community," Office of the Director of National

Intelligence, Testimony before the Senate Select Committee on Intelligence, January 29, 2014, p. 6, http://www.intelligence.senate.gov/140129/clapper.pdf.

27. Id.

28. James R. Clapper, "Worldwide Threat Assessment of the U.S. Intelligence Community." Office of the Director of National Intelligence, Testimony before the Senate Select Committee on Intelligence, February 26, 2015, http://www.dni.gov/files/documents/Unclassified_2015_ATA_SFR_-_SASC_FINAL.pdf.

29. Riyadh Mohammed, "How Iran Is Taking Over the Middle East," *Fiscal Times*, March 18, 2015, http://www.thefiscaltimes.com/2015/03/18/How-Iran-Taking-Over-Middle-East.

30. James R. Clapper, "Worldwide Threat Assessment of the U.S. Intelligence Community," Office of the Director of National Intelligence, Testimony before the Senate Select Committee on Intelligence, January 29, 2014, p. 6, http://www.intelligence.senate.gov/140129/clapper.pdf.

31. Jeremy Page, "China Warns North Korean Nuclear Threat Is Rising," *Wall Street Journal*, April 22, 2015, http://www.wsj.com/articles/china-warns-north-korean-nuclear-threat-is-rising-1429745706.

32. James R. Clapper, "Worldwide Threat Assessment of the U.S. Intelligence Community," Office of the Director of National Intelligence, Testimony before the Senate Select Committee on Intelligence, January 29, 2014, p. 5, http://www.intelligence.senate.gov/140129/clapper.pdf.

33. "National Security Strategy of the United States," White House, January 1987, p. 7, nssarchive.us/NSSR/1987.pdf.

34. Clapper, January 29, 2014, pp. 4–5.

35. Id., pp. 19–21.

36. See, for example, Hassan Hassan, "Islamic terror group rose to power by filling the void created by political and religious chaos," *Daily Telegraph*, August 23, 2014.

37. James R. Clapper, "Worldwide Threat Assessment of the U.S. Intelligence Community." Office of the Director of National Intelligence, Testimony before the Senate Select Committee on Intelligence, January 29, 2014, p. 19, http://www.intelligence .senate.gov/140129/clapper.pdf.

38. www.globalsecurity.org/military/world/para/al-qaida.htm.

39. Miles Amoore and Richard Kerbaj, "Jihadist plot to grab Iran's nuclear secrets," *Sunday Times*, October 5, 2014, http://www .thesundaytimes.co.uk/sto/news/world_news/Middle_East/article 1467470.ece.

40. Harald Doornbos and Jenan Moussa, "Found: The Islamic State's Terror Laptop of Doom," *Foreign Relations*, August 28, 2014, http://foreignpolicy.com/2014/08/28/found-the-islamic-states -terror-laptop-of-doom/#_.

41. Id.

42. Id.

43. Id.

44. Id.

45. "Between the Millstones: The State of Iraq's Minorities Since the Fall of Mosul," Minority Rights Group International, February 2015, http://minorityrights.org/13031/reports/MRG_Rep_Iraq _ONLINE.pdf.

46. Dennis C. Blair, "Written Responses to Questions from the Committee," Before the Senate Select Committee on Intelligence, February 12, 2009, http://www.cnn.com/2015/01/11/politics /feinstein-visa-program-is-achilles-heel-of-america/; Michael McCaul, "Islamic State Is Recruiting America's 'Jihadi Cool'

Crowd," *Wall Street Journal*, September 11, 2014, http://www.wsj
.com/articles/michael-mccall-islamic-state-is-recruiting-amer
icas-jihadi-cool-crowd-1410478638; http://cnsnews.com/news
/article/hundreds-soldiers-hezbollah-inside-us-says-homeland
-security-chairman.

47. Edwin Mora, "'Hundreds' of 'Soldiers of Hezbollah' Inside the
U.S., Says Homeland Security Chairman," CNS News, March
23, 2012, http://cnsnews.com/news/article/hundreds-soldiers
-hezbollah-inside-us-says-homeland-security-chairman; Arthur
Brice, "Iran, Hezbollah mine Latin America for revenue, recruits,
analysis says," CNN, June 3, 2013.

48. Eric Bradner, "Feinstein: Visa program is 'Achilles heel,'" CNN,
January 11, 2015, http://www.cnn.com/2015/01/11/politics/fein
stein-visa-program-is-achilles-heel-of-america/.

49. Robert Wright, "ISIS and the Forgotten, Deadly Threat of
Homegrown Terrorism," *Atlantic*, September 19, 2014, http://
www.theatlantic.com/politics/archive/2014/09/will-obamas-isis
-strategy-actually-worsen-the-terror-threat/380465/.

50. Susan Jones, "FBI Director: 'I Have Home-Grown Violent Extremist Investigations in Every Single State," CNSnews.com,
February 26, 2015, http://cnsnews.com/print/891828.

51. David Bailey, "Six Minnesota men charged with conspiring to
support Islamic State," Reuters, April 20, 2015, http://af.reuters
.com/articlePrint?articleId=AFL1N0XH11920150420.

52. "Muslim Americans: No Sign of Growth in Alienation or Support for Extremism," Pew Research Center, August 2011, http://
www.people-press.org/files/legacy-pdf/Muslim%20American%20
Report%2010-02-12%20fix.pdf.

53. Id.

54. Id., p. 65.

55. Id.

56. Id.

57. Id., p. 68.

58. Id., p. 70.

59. Murphy, p. 38.

60. Id.

61. Id.

62. Id., p. 39.

63. Clapper, January 29, 2014, p. 7; Bill Gertz, "U.S. Opposes New Draft Treaty from China and Russia Banning Space Weapons," *Free Beacon*, June 19, 2014, http://freebeacon.com/national -security/u-s-opposes-new-draft-treaty-from-china-and-russia -banning-space-weapons/.

64. Murphy, p. 40.

65. Id.

66. Id.

67. Lee Rainie, Janna Anderson, and Jennifer Connolly, "Cyber Attacks Likely to Increase," Pew Research Internet Project, October 29, 2014, http://www.pewinternet.org/2014/10/29 /cyber-attacks-likely-to-increase/#themes-among-those-who -expect-yes-there-will-be-major-cyber-attacks.

68. Id.

69. www.cnn.com/2015/06/04/politics/federal-agency-hacked -personnel-management/index.html.

70. http://www.theatlantic.com/national/archive/2015/06/federal -data-hacking-worse/395807/.

71. "Ensuring a Strong U.S. Defense for the Future: The National Defense Panel Review of the 2014 Quadrennial Defense Review,"

United States Institute for Peace, July 31, 2014, http://www.usip
.org/sites/default/files/Ensuring-a-Strong-U.S.-Defense-for-the
-Future-NDP-Review-of-the-QDR.pdf.

72. Id., p. viii.

73. Id., p. 52.

74. Id.

75. Id., p. x.

76. P. W. Singer, Heather Messera, and Brendan Orino, "D.C.'s New Guard: What Does the Next Generation of American Leaders Think?" Foreign Policy at Brookings, February 2011, p. 14, http://www.brookings.edu/~/media/research/files /reports/2011/2/young%20leaders%20singer/02_young _leaders_singer.pdf.

77. Id.

78. Id., p. 89.

79. Bruce Drake,. "Plurality of Americans support current level of defense spending," Pew Research Center, February 24, 2014, http://www.pewresearch.org/fact-tank/2014/02/24/plurality-of -americans-support-current-level-of-defense-spending/.

80. "2013 Demographics: Profile of the Military Community," Department of Defense, p. iv, http://www.militaryonesource .mil/12038/MOS/Reports/2013-Demographics-Report.pdf.

81. Ronald Reagan, "Address Accepting the Presidential Nomination at the Republican National Convention in Detroit," The American Presidency Project, July 17, 1980, http://www .presidency.ucsb.edu/ws/?pid=25970.

## 10. On the Constitution

1. Benjamin Franklin, *Writings* (New York: Penguin, 1997), p. 1140.

2. Joseph Story, *The Miscellaneous Writings—Literary, Critical,*

*Juridical, and Political of Joseph Story, Now First Collected* (Ithaca, NY: Cornell University Library, 2009), p. 150.

3. Id., p. 151.

4. Id., p. 152.

5. Id., pp. 155–56.

6. Charles de Montesquieu, *The Spirit of the Laws*, Anne M. Cohler, Basia C. Miller, and Harold S. Stone, eds. (Cambridge, U.K.: Cambridge University Press, 2009), Part 1, Book 1, Chapter 2.

7. Id., Part 1, Book 3, Chapter 3.

8. Id., Part 2, Book 2, Chapter 6.

9. James Madison, *The Federalist No. 47* (New York: Signet Classics, 2003), p. 298.

10. Id., p. 300.

11. John Locke, *The Second Treatise of Government*, Chapter 11, Sec. 141 (New York: Barnes & Noble, 2004).

12. Id.

13. Karl Marx and Friedrich Engels, *The Communist Manifesto* (London: Soho, 2010), p. 36.

14. Michelle Obama, Public Remarks, May 14, 2008, https://www.youtube.com/watch?v=4f2j_a_7XkE.

15. Barack Obama, Public Remarks, October 20, 2008, https://www.youtube.com/watch?v=KrefKCaV8m4.

16. Mark R. Levin, *Liberty and Tyranny* (New York: Simon & Schuster, 2008), p. 193.

17. Alexis de Tocqueville, *Democracy in America*, Henry Reeve, trans., Phillips Bradley, ed., vol. I (New York: Library of America, 2004), p. 319.

18. Mark R. Levin, *The Liberty Amendments* (New York: Simon & Schuster, 2013), p. 3.

19. Id., pp. 3–4.

20. Clyde Wayne Crews, "CEI's 2015 Unconstitutionality Index: 27 Regulations for Every Law," Competitive Enterprise Institute, January 4, 2015, https://cei.org/blog/ceis-2015-unconstitution ality-index-27-regulations-every-law.

21. Federal Register, Vol. 79, No. 250, Wednesday, December 31, 2014, https://www.federalregister.gov/articles/2014/12/31.

22. Office of the Federal Register, "Federal Register Pages Published 1936–2013," https://www.federalregister.gov/uploads/2014/04 /OFR-STATISTICS-CHARTS-ALL1-1-1-2013.pdf.

23. Office of the Federal Register, "Annual Percentage Change 1976–2013," https://www.federalregister.gov/uploads/2014/04 /OFR-STATISTICS-CHARTS-ALL1-1-1-2013.pdf; Clyde Wayne Crews, "CEI's 2015 Unconstitutionality Index: 27 Regulations for Every Law," Competitive Enterprise Institute, January 4, 2015, https://cei.org/blog/ceis-2015-unconstitution ality-index-27-regulations-every-law.

24. Woodrow Wilson, *Constitutional Government in the United States* (New York: Columbia University Press, 1908), p. 16.

25. Tyler Hartsfield and Grace-Marie Turner, "48 Changes to ObamaCare . . . So Far," Galen Institute, February 25, 2015, http://www.galen.org/assets/48-Changes-so-far-to-ObamaCare1 .pdf.

26. 75 Fed. Reg. 31,514, "Prevention of Significant Deterioration and Title V Greenhouse Gas Tailoring Rule."

27. Laurence Tribe, "Professor Tribe Takes Obama to School," *Wall Street Journal*, December 6, 2014, A12.

28. Laurence Tribe, "The Clean Power Plan Is Unconstitutional," *Wall Street Journal*, December 23, 2014, A13.

29. 79 Fed. Reg. 22,188, "Proposed Definition of 'Waters of the United States' Under the Clean Water Act."

30. Michael D. Shear and Julia Preston, "Obama Pushed 'Fullest Extent' of His Powers on Immigration Plan," *New York Times*, November 28, 2014, http://www.nytimes.com/2014/11/29/us /white-house-tested-limits-of-powers-before-action-on-immigra tion.html?_r=1.

31. Robert Rector, "The Fiscal Consequences of Executive Amnesty," Testimony before the Committee on Oversight and Government Reform, United States House of Representatives, March 17, 2015, http://oversight.house.gov/wp-content/uploads/2015/03 /Mr.-Rector-Testimony-Bio-TNT.pdf.

32. *State of Texas* v. *United States of America*, No. 14-254, slip op. at 111 (S.D. Tx. Feb. 16, 2015).

33. Barack Obama, "Interview With HuffPost," March 21, 2015, http://www.huffingtonpost.com/2015/03/21/obama-huffpost -interview-transcript_n_6905450.html?ncid=tweetlnkushpmg 00000067.

34. George Washington, "Washington's Farewell Address 1796," The Avalon Project Documents in Law, History and Diplomacy, http://avalon.law.yale.edu/18th_century/washing.asp.

**Epilogue: A New Civil Rights Movement**

1. Ronald Reagan, "Farewell Speech." January 11, 1989, http:// reagan2020.us/speeches/Farewell.asp.

2. Thomas Jefferson, "Letter to Wilson Cary Nicholas, September 7, 1803." *Thomas Jefferson: Writings: Autobiography/Notes on the State of Virginia/Public and Private Papers/Addresses/Letters*, Merrill D. Peterson, ed. (New York: Library of America, 1984), p. 1140.

3. Samuel Adams, "Letter from Candidus," *Boston Gazette*, October 7, 1771. Appearing in *American Patriotism: Speeches*,

*Letters, And Other Papers Which Illustrate The Foundation, The Development, The Preservation of the United States of America,* Selim H. Peabody, ed. (New York: American Book Exchange, 1880), p. 32.

4. Mark R. Levin, *Liberty and Tyranny* (New York: Simon & Schuster, 2009), p. 195.

5. See id., pp. 193–205, for further guidance.

6. See id., pp. 199–205, and Mark R. Levin, *The Liberty Amendments* (New York: Simon & Schuster, 2013).

7. Frederic Bastiat, *The Law* (Filiquarian Publishing, 2005), p. 71.

**Acknowledgments**

1. Ronald Reagan, *A Time for Choosing: The Speeches of Ronald Reagan—1961–1982* (Chicago: Regnery Gateway, 1983), 57.